FRENCH COUNTRY LIGHT

COOKING

FRENCH COUNTRY LIGHT
COOKING

By Evelyne Slomon

A JOHN BOSWELL ASSOCIATES/KING HILL PRODUCTIONS BOOK

A PERIGEE BOOK

Perigee Books
are published by
The Putnam Publishing Group
200 Madison Avenue
New York, NY 10016

Library of Congress Cataloging-in-Publication Data

Slomon, Evelyne.
   French country light cooking : easy, healthy, low-calorie recipes
from cassoulet to coq au vin / by Evelyne Slomon.
     p. cm.
   "A Perigee Book"
   Includes index.
   ISBN 0-399-51816-9 (alk. paper)
    1. Cookery, French. 2. Low-calorie diet—Recipes. I. Title.
TX719.S565 1993   92-41332
641.5944—dc20   CIP

Design by Nan Jernigan/The Colman Press
Cover illustration and design by Richard Rossiter
Printed in the United States of America

1 2 3 4 5 6 7 8 9 10

This book is printed on acid-free paper.

For Eleanor Triboletti, my good friend
and trusted "sous"—without whose help
this project would surely have been
"in the weeds" and a whole lot less fun . . .

CONTENTS

Introduction   11

About the Nutritional Numbers   13

About the Ingredients   14

A Note About Technique   17

Chapter 1   HORS D'OEUVRES   19

Excite your appetite the French way with tempting light starters, such as Marinated Lentils, Artichokes Stuffed Niçoise Style, Herbed Chèvre Spread, Wild Mushroom Ragout Tartines and Salmon Rillettes.

Chapter 2   SOUPS   43

Healthful and comforting, these are vegetable-based soups—*potages*—to start a meal or complete a light lunch. Creamy Carrot Soup, Gratinéed Onion Soup, Soupe au Pistou and Chilled Tomato Soup with Mint, Herbed Croutons and Feta Cheese are just a few.

Chapter 3   **SALADS AND COLD ENTREES**   59

Appetizer salads, composed salads and main-course salads are featured here, along with innovative, low-calorie dressings with flavors like lemon Dijon, sherry shallot, orange-thyme, bacon and calvados and roasted walnut.

Chapter 4   **FISH AND SHELLFISH**   81

Quick-cooking and light, seafood offers great variety with few calories. Dine delectably on Halibut en Papillote with Lemon, Broiled Sole à L'Orange, Baked Red Snapper Catalane, Bouillabaisse, Shrimp and Scallop Mousse with Watercress Cream and more.

Chapter 5   **CHICKEN AND MEATS**   109

Coq au Vin, Pan-Roasted Duck Breasts à l'Orange with Shallot Confit, Steak au Poivre, even Cassoulet of White Beans with Lamb, Pork and Sausage will surprise you with their savory slimness.

Chapter 6   **VEGETABLES**   129

From the French garden come taste and variety *extraordinaire* in dishes such as Carrots Provençal with sweet Vermouth and Fennel, Roasted Potato Slices with Garlic and Herbs and Spinach with Lemon Confit and Olives.

Chapter 7   PASTA, RICE AND BEANS   153

A sampling of side dishes and meatless main courses that keep within calorie limits while they expand the boundaries of flavor: Thin Noodles with Pistou and Roasted Tomatoes, Couscous Marinière and Red Beans, Chicken and Pumpkin Piperade.

Chapter 8   DESSERTS   167

Spectacular is the only word for these extraordinary sweets. It's hard to believe that recipes like Chocolate Mousse, Apple Soufflé Cake, Fruit Gratin with Sugar Nut Crust and Pear Soufflé with Raspberry Coulis can be so light.

Introduction

"Light" French cooking might seem a contradiction in terms to most. Many are not aware that there exists two distinct forms of cooking in France: *haute cuisine*—as practiced by French chefs and eaten on rare occasions in fancy restaurants; and everyday French country cooking—as practiced in the home and eaten by everyone else. Face it, the average French person doesn't dine on foie gras, truffles and pheasant under glass on any given night. In fact, everyday French country cuisine is the antithesis of the rich extravagance and theatrics of *haute cuisine.* The philosophy of the home cook is to *faites simple,* "make it simple."

When I was a child in France, we shopped for food every day and cooked according to the season. As a family, we looked forward to the rituals that each season afforded. We delighted in the simple pleasures of *fraise des bois au naturelle,* tiny wild strawberries, in the spring and *cèpes,* wild mushrooms, sautéed with garlic and parsley, in the fall. For fancy cooking with exotic ingredients, the option of the restaurant was always available. French country cooking is not restaurant cooking: it is restorative and nurturing; it is the continual celebration of the bountiful raw ingredients of France.

Traditional French cuisine is constantly evolving from century to century and decade to decade. French food and dining habits are not what they were in the nineteenth century, they are not what they were during the fifties and they are not what they were in the seventies or even the indulgent eighties. Dishes and their preparations are always being revised. In the nineteenth and twentieth centuries, French cooking embraced foreign influences; Italian and Spanish overtones in the south, and Moroccan and Vietnamese in the urban areas. Such ingredients as couscous, coriander, cilantro, saffron, harissa, ginger, chilies, sesame, tofu, rice noodles, olive oil, tomatoes, pesto, pasta, sweet pimientos, almonds and cayenne have only enriched the French repertoire.

Today the French are just as health- and diet-conscious as Americans, but they don't think about it in the same way. French people believe that it is their God given right to eat well—every day. Furthermore, they consider this essential to their well-being. From the French point of view, eating well is equated with watching out for one's welfare by eating more healthfully. It is typically American to associate deprivation and guilt with eating, but because the French "exist to eat" and "don't eat to exist," they tend to look upon eating nutritiously as a challenge and not a limitation.

It is from this philosophy that I have carried out, in the following pages, recipes that are naturally low in calories and percentage of fat, while still preserving the authentic flavors of the original dishes. While I have not set out to write a diet or nutrition book, I have taken into account all current nutritional concerns in developing these dishes. However, this collection of recipes has been created to delight the senses, to comfort and to nourish the body and the soul. Most of them reflect our busy lifestyles and are quick and easy to assemble. They all contain exact calorie counts and percentage of calories from fat, to take the guess work out of planning meals, and they have been trimmed down and lightened up as much as possible without giving up flavor. Butter, flour and cream have been kept to a minimum throughout. In fact, not a single drop of cream and less than 1½ sticks of butter are employed in the preparation of all the more than 165 recipes in this book.

A diet, or *régime* in France, is looked upon as a medicinal treatment. And I agree. One cannot be "on a diet" for the rest of one's life, but we can learn to live and eat lighter and better. Perhaps a change in philosophy, to a more French point of view, might not be such a farfetched notion. If we learn to take better care of ourselves, nourishing our bodies and, in turn, our spirits, some of that famous French *joie de vivre,* "joy of life," might just rub off on us.

About the Nutritional Numbers

All the recipes in *French Country Light Cooking* were developed with a reduced-calorie eating plan for an average healthy adult in mind. The maximum number of calories allowed were: 200 for first courses, whether appetizers, soups or starter salads; 400 for main courses; 175 for side, including vegetables, grains and breads; and 250 for desserts. Counts for many of the recipes in this book fall well below the maximum, which allows a great deal of freedom and diversity in menu planning.

Today's most up-to-date nutritional guidelines recommend that as a general rule no more than 30 percent of calories ingested come from fats. To help accomplish this goal, we've listed the percentage of calories from fat along with the calories per serving at the beginning of each recipe.

Many of the percentages here are low, but some do rise above 30 percent. Don't turn away; all these recipes contain very little fat. The perceptual problem comes when an exceptionally low-calorie dish contains even a little oil. For example, a lettuce salad with vinaigrette dressing made with a bare minimum of oil will have a high percentage of calories from fat because lettuce has exceptionally few calories and oil contains 40 calories per teaspoon. Also, since some foods, even nutritionally sound foods like fish, are naturally high in oils, it is impossible that every dish you eat meet this guideline. The important thing to remember is that 30 percent of all your calories from fat *over a two- or three-day period* should be no more than 30 percent. Just as with calorie counting, it is the total of all the foods you eat that is meaningful.

About the Ingredients

As a classically trained French chef, I am always particularly pleased to recall the little "trucs" (things-tricks) my family taught me and to use them in my work. Cooking for them is instinctual and intuitive. They know nothing about chemistry and calories, but they sure know how to extract the most from the least. From the very beginning, I learned to eat and cook in this manner and to appreciate food that tastes of what it is. This aspect of my cooking is very significant throughout this book, because the ingredients are pared down to the essentials. Therefore, the essentials must be the best that they can be.

HERBS—The most popular herbs in French cooking are parsley, thyme, bay leaf, mint, rosemary, chives, chervil and sage. Do try to use fresh herbs whenever possible. At the very least, fresh parsley is readily available all year. Some fresh herbs, such as parsley, chives, rosemary and basil should be avoided in their dried states. On the other hand, dried thyme, bay leaf, tarragon and sage are perfectly fine. A sprinkling of fresh parsley, chives or basil over a dish just before serving isn't just for looks; it is at that moment that the herb will have its most intense flavoring impact.

SPICES—Spices such as fennel seed, coriander seed, cumin, caraway, juniper berry and cloves are best ground just before using. Grinding them at the last minute releases their delicious flavor and scent far more efficiently throughout the dish. This is especially important when flavor is derived from spices and herbs instead of fats.

PEPPER—Freshly ground black pepper is a must in any good cooking.

SALT—Use salt sparingly, and when you do, try to use natural sea salt.

OILS—I have pared down the choices of oils in this book to olive oil, extra virgin olive oil and Asian sesame oil. Use any good-quality pure olive oil for most of the dishes. For those that call for a little more distinctive olive taste, extra virgin olive oil is preferred. I like French extra virgin olive oil from Provence, which is extremely elegant and fruity.

Walnut oil is another French favorite. Unfortunately, it's expensive and not very much in demand for general cooking, so it will probably go rancid from nonuse on your shelf. I often opt for an oil blend that calls for 1 part Asian sesame oil to 2 parts olive oil. The result is a mellow nutty flavor that is very close to good-quality French walnut oil.

If you don't use your oils regularly, store them in the refrigerator. If the oil should solidify in the bottle, simply leave it out at room temperature and the clouds will disappear when the oil warms up.

VINEGARS—Vinegars are essential flavorings to any light cuisine as they are virtually calorie-free. The French are big on vinegars; they use them liberally in salads, sauces, soups, stews and vegetables. Red wine vinegar should be at least 5% acidity to be good; otherwise it's cut with water. Champagne vinegar is a very fine light vinegar, as is cider vinegar, which is slightly sweet. Sherry wine vinegar is sweet and full-bodied, as is balsamic vinegar. Raspberry vinegar has an intense berry flavor and beautiful color.

CHEESES—Gruyère with its mild nutty flavor is the favored melting cheese of France. Swiss cheese can be substituted, if necessary. Goat cheese, or *chèvre* in French, is a mild, tangy, slightly creamy cheese that is lower in fat than cow's milk cheeses. It is available both domestically and imported from France. French feta from Corsica is creamier and less salty than the Greek version. Use it on salads, soups and in cooking.

BREAD CRUMBS—Most recipes call for unseasoned plain bread crumbs, which can be purchased in the supermarket. If you want to make your own: Cut a few ¼-inch-thick slices of stale bread and crisp them in a preheated 400° F. oven for about 10 minutes, or until lightly colored. Break the slices up and grind them in a food processor. They will keep in an airtight container in the refrigerator for several weeks.

BACON—When used sparingly as a condiment, nothing compares with the subtle smoky flavor bacon lends to a dish. This flavor is essential to many country French dishes. Use lean slab or thick sliced bacon. Because I use bacon so sparingly, I keep the package frozen and defrost one slice at a time whenever I need one. A thick (¼-inch) slice of lean bacon equals approximately 1 ounce. Always blanch the bacon in boiling water for 30 seconds before using; this removes some of the fat and extra salt.

BROTHS—Most of the recipes in this book call for using reduced-sodium chicken broth, which is in many cases cut with water. If you are vegetarian, there are canned vegetable broths available as well. Most everyday cooking in France does not employ complicated stocks as a base. Simple broths whether homemade or canned usually suffice. This tends to fit in with the busy lifestyle of today's families both here and in France.

WINES AND SPIRITS—In most cases, I prefer using white vermouth in cooking to dry white wine as it has so much more flavor and is inexpensive. Red vermouth is sweet and can be used as a substitute for sherry, port or marsala. Pernod or Ricard are anise-based liquors popular in the South of France for drinking and cooking. Calvados is brandy made from apples; applejack or domestic apple brandy can be substituted for it. Any inexpensive brandy from Spain or California can be used to replace Cognac. Rich-flavored dark rum, such as Myers's, is generally best for cooking. *Eau de vie* is a clear distilled spirit. Many of these, such as pear William (pear), kirsch (cherry) or framboise (raspberry), are used in desserts.

A Note About Technique

FOIL "SAUTÉ" AND FOIL "ROASTING": Foil "sauté" is a technique that uses a minimum of fat: vegetables sweat under a piece of foil. The method is simple. A small amount—no more than 1 tablespoon—of olive oil is heated in a skillet and the thinly sliced or diced vegetables are added. A sheet of foil is pressed down directly onto the vegetables and they are cooked over medium heat, and stirred only occasionally, until they are lightly colored and tender. Why not just cover the pot? Because the heat from the vegetables forms condensation on the inside of the lid, which produces steam. When the foil is pushed directly down on top of the vegetables, no condensation forms and the vegetables are able to brown and tenderize more easily. The foil merely helps retain the natural moisture in the food without adding liquid to the dish. Wrapping vegetables, meat and fish in a foil packet and roasting them creates a similar situation—a kind of dry-steam roasting. The results are tender, juicy and best of all, very low in fat.

THICKENING: Traditionally most French stews, ragouts, soups and sauces were thickened with a flour- and butter-based roux. I have found that when I add a very small amount of flour without any fat to the stew, soup or sauce *before* the liquid is stirred in, I am able to create a sauce with as much body and flavor as with the heavier roux bases. The flour must be evenly sprinkled over the food and stirred until no trace of white appears. This prevents lumping and assures that the flour will cook evenly throughout.

Chapter One

HORS D'OEUVRES

The hors d'oeuvre course's purpose in the scheme of a typical, three-course French country meal is to excite the appetite. The word itself means "outside" of the main "work," or event—the entree. An hors d'oeuvre is supposed to prepare diners for the main course, not fill them up. That is why so many traditional hors d'oeuvres are light, marinated vegetables known as *crudités*. A far cry from our notion of a bunch of carrot and celery sticks with French onion soup mix dip, these *crudités* sparkle like gems, and their refreshing flavors are a virtual dieter's delight. Serve single portions, garnished with a lettuce leaf, as a simple appetizer, or in a double portion as a light lunch. For a dinner party or buffet, prepare a selection. Some *crudités,* such as Pickled Red Onions and Chiffonade of Red Cabbage, are not really meant to be plated on their own. Serve them as part of an assortment of *crudités,* or as a condiment with fish and meats, or as a garnish with salads.

I've also included some delicious dips, such as Sherry Dijon Dressing and Eggplant Caviar, and spreads, such as Herbed Chèvre and Salmon Rillettes. Substitute paper-thin slices of vegetable for high-fat potato or corn chips, and feel free to indulge yourself. These dishes are perfect for the party table, and they are so tasty it's hard to believe they are low in calories, too.

Other more formal hors d'oeuvres, such as Mixed Wild Mushroom and Field Mushroom Salad, Cucumber Barquettes Filled with Tapenade, Citrus "Cooked" Salmon on a Bed of Fresh Herbs, Provençal Marinated Vegetable Sandwich and Wild Mushroom Ragout Tartines could easily stand in for a satisfying light lunch.

For more appetizer selections, turn to Salads and Cold Entrees (page 59) and try some of the lighter salads such as Asparagus, Endive and Orange Salad with Raspberry Vinaigrette; Corsican Tomato, Cucumber, Mint and Feta Salad or Fresh Fennel, Orange and Olive Salad with Gruyère Cheese. The Vegetables chapter (page 129) is also a good source. In it you'll find side dishes such as Zucchini Barquettes Filled with Olives, Onion and Tomato; Artichokes à la Barigoule with Tomatoes and Thyme and Ratatouille that, when served chilled, are superb appetizers.

One of my favorite meals consists of a small plate of Poached Leeks with Plum Tomatoes and Dijon Vinaigrette, a nice hunk of warm, crusty French bread for dipping in the dressing and a glass of a good sturdy Côtes du Rhône. This is light French country dining at its best.

Artichokes Stuffed Niçoise Style

4 SERVINGS   36% CALORIES FROM FAT   196 CALORIES PER SERVING

1 slice of lean bacon, cut into ¼-inch dice
4 medium artichokes (8 ounces each)
1 tablespoon olive oil
1 medium onion, chopped
4 garlic cloves, minced
8 sprigs of fresh thyme or ½ teaspoon dried thyme leaves
2 plum tomatoes, peeled, seeded and chopped
1 tablespoon chopped parsley
½ cup plain bread crumbs
1 lemon, thinly sliced into rounds
2 cans (14½ ounces each) reduced-sodium chicken broth

1. Preheat the oven to 400° F. Bring a small saucepan of water to a boil. Add the bacon and cook 30 seconds. Drain and rinse briefly under running water. Pat dry on a paper towel.

2. Trim off the artichoke stems so they can stand upright. Cut off 1 to 2 inches from the tops and bend back and pull off the tough outer leaves. With a spoon, preferably a sharp grapefruit spoon, scoop out and discard the hairy choke in the center.

3. In a medium nonstick skillet, heat the olive oil. Add the onion, garlic and bacon, cover and cook 2 minutes. Uncover and continue to cook, stirring occasionally, until the onions are tender and the bacon is lightly browned, 3 to 5 minutes longer.

4. Add the thyme, tomatoes, parsley and bread crumbs and mix well. Stuff the centers of the artichokes with the bread crumb filling.

5. Place the lemon slices on the bottom of a high-sided baking dish or soufflé dish just large enough to hold the artichokes in a single layer. Add the stuffed artichokes, pour the broth into the dish and add enough water to come ¾ up the sides of the dish.

6. Cover the dish tightly with foil and bake 1½ hours, or until the artichokes are very tender. Remove from the baking dish and let cool to room temperature before serving.

Asparagus with Sherry Dijon Dressing

French cooks have been experimenting with healthy tofu just like Americans. Here's an example of when East meets West—French country-style. I think you'll find yourself using this dressing over and over again, not just on asparagus, but with broccoli, carrots and string beans as well. Try it as a dip for crudités.

4 SERVINGS   36% CALORIES FROM FAT   71 CALORIES PER SERVING

1¼ to 1½ pounds asparagus spears, to yield 1 pound trimmed
2 tablespoons sherry wine vinegar
1 tablespoon Dijon mustard
8 ounces soft tofu (½ package), drained
1 teaspoon Asian sesame oil or walnut oil
⅛ teaspoon salt
⅛ teaspoon freshly ground pepper
1 tablespoon chopped chives

1. Cut off the tough, woody stems from the asparagus. In a large skillet, bring about 1 inch of water to a boil. Add the asparagus and cook until fork tender, about 3 minutes. Drain into a colander.

2. In a blender or food processor, whip the vinegar, mustard and tofu together. Add the oil in a thin stream. Season with the salt and pepper.

3. To serve, arrange the asparagus spears on a serving platter and spoon the dressing over them. Sprinkle the chives on top. Serve warm or at room temperature.

Maltaise Variation

Prepare the recipe for Asparagus with Sherry Dijon Dressing as described above, but in step 2, substitute 2 tablespoons raspberry vinegar for the sherry wine vinegar and 1 teaspoon walnut oil for the sesame oil. Add 1 teaspoon minced orange zest along with the salt and pepper.

Beets with Raspberry Vinegar

These pickled beets are an absolute must for any crudité plate. The micro-wave speeds up cooking and gives excellent results; of course, the beets may also be baked or boiled. Their natural sweetness compliments the raspberry vinegar. It's hard to believe all that flavor could be so low in calories. Slice or cube the beets and add a colorful touch to salads, or serve the beets on their own with a little chopped garlic, fresh parsley and a few drops of extra virgin olive oil or walnut oil.

4 SERVINGS   2% CALORIES FROM FAT   52 CALORIES PER SERVING

1½ pounds beets (about 8 medium)
¼ cup raspberry vinegar
Salt and freshly ground pepper to taste

1. Cut the roots and stems from the beets. Place in a glass pie plate with ¼ cup water. Cover with microwave-safe plastic wrap and pierce to allow the steam to escape.

2. Microwave on High 15 minutes, rotating the plate after 7 minutes. Test for doneness and cook up to 5 minutes longer, until the beets are tender in the center when pierced with a small knife.

3. As soon as the beets are cool enough to handle, remove the skins. Cut the beets into thin slices or ½-inch cubes.

4. In a medium bowl, toss the beets with the vinegar, salt and pepper. Cover and refrigerate, tossing occasionally, about 2 hours before serving.

Chiffonade of Red Cabbage

Alsace in the northeast of France is noted for its red cabbage dishes. In this version of "slaw," the cabbage is tenderized by the vinegar and sugar. This beautiful low-calorie vegetable makes a colorful addition to a crudité plate, it goes well with Marinated Lentils (page 32) and makes a fine side salad with almost any sandwich.

8 SERVINGS   6% CALORIES FROM FAT   42 CALORIES PER SERVING

1 small head of red cabbage (2 pounds), trimmed
⅓ cup raspberry vinegar
2 tablespoons lemon juice
2 tablespoons sugar
1 teaspoon caraway seeds, crushed or ground in a spice grinder
½ teaspoon salt
¼ teaspoon freshly ground pepper

1. Using a large stainless steel knife, halve the cabbage head and cut out the thick core. Cut the cabbage into very thin slices or shred it in a food processor using the fine cutting blade.

2. In a large bowl, toss the shredded cabbage, vinegar, lemon juice, sugar, caraway, salt and pepper until well mixed.

3. Cover with plastic wrap and marinate in the refrigerator at least 4 hours, or overnight, before serving.

Shredded Sweet and Sour Carrot Salad

What a great way to dress up raw carrots. Try this refreshing crunchy salad mixed into a green salad or as a sandwich topping.

4 SERVINGS   3% CALORIES FROM FAT   28 CALORIES PER SERVING

8 medium carrots (1 pound), peeled and trimmed
¼ cup lemon juice
2 tablespoons sugar
¼ teaspoon cinnamon

1. Shred the carrots in a food processor using the appropriate blade, or grate them on the large holes of a four-sided hand grater.

2. In a medium bowl, toss the carrots, lemon juice, sugar and cinnamon together until the carrots are well coated.

3. Cover the bowl with plastic wrap and refrigerate 2 hours, or until chilled, before serving.

— *Roasted Whole Garlic with Fresh Thyme* —

Roasting brings out the mellow sweetness of garlic. Try this nearly fat-free treat hot or cold spread on toasted bread, mixed with vegetables or in a baked potato instead of a pat of butter.

4 SERVINGS   4% CALORIES FROM FAT   154 CALORIES PER SERVING

4 large heads of garlic, trimmed to expose the tops of the cloves
¾ cup reduced-sodium chicken broth
8 sprigs of fresh thyme or ½ teaspoon dried thyme leaves
Salt and freshly ground pepper

1. Preheat the oven to 400° F. Place the garlic heads in a small, shallow baking dish just large enough to fit them snugly.

2. Pour the chicken broth over the garlic. Place the thyme sprigs over each garlic head and season lightly with salt and pepper.

3. Cover tightly with foil and bake 1 hour, or until each clove is soft to the touch when tested with the tip of a knife. Serve with some of the cooking juices spooned over each bulb.

Herbed Chèvre Spread with Cucumbers and Lemon Honey Dressing

This delicious and unusual light hors d'oeuvre is a version of *"cabichou,"* a soft goat cheese spread popular in the south of France. It is equally good as a dessert served with thin slices of apple or pear. "Chips" of thinly sliced cucumber, apple or pear allow you to dip without guilt. Personally, I enjoy this cheese mixture spread on toast as a breakfast treat.

8 SERVINGS   45% CALORIES FROM FAT   123 CALORIES PER SERVING

1 recipe Herbed Chèvre Spread (recipe follows)
1 tablespoon lemon juice
1 tablespoon honey
1 medium seedless hothouse cucumber, thinly sliced
Cracked black pepper

1. Mound the cheese spread in the center of a large round plate.

2. In a small bowl, combine the lemon juice and honey. Stir until the dressing is well blended.

3. Arrange the cucumber slices in overlapping circles around the cheese. Pour the dressing over the cheese and sprinkle some cracked black pepper on top.

Herbed Chèvre Spread

MAKES ABOUT 2 CUPS   50% CALORIES FROM FAT   28 CALORIES PER TABLESPOON

6 ounces goat cheese (1 small log)
8 ounces nonfat cream cheese
¼ cup nonfat plain yogurt
2 garlic cloves, crushed through a press
1 teaspoon fresh thyme leaves or ½ teaspoon dried
1 tablespoon chopped chives
Salt and freshly ground pepper

1. In a food processor, whip the goat cheese, cream cheese, yogurt and garlic until well blended. Fold in the thyme and chives by hand. (Do not overmix, or the spread will turn into "green" cheese!) Season with salt and pepper to taste.

2. Scoop the mixture into a crock or serving bowl and refrigerate about 4 hours, or until chilled and slightly stiffened.

Cucumbers with Mint and Champagne Vinaigrette

Cucumbers and mint are exceptionally cool and delicious as part of a crudité plate or served with pickled beets (page 23). If champagne vinegar is unavailable, any white wine vinegar or cider vinegar can be substituted. I prefer seedless hothouse, or English, cucumbers to the standard kind because they are more digestible. They needn't be seeded and peeling is optional.

4 SERVINGS   67% CALORIES FROM FAT   44 CALORIES PER SERVING

> *2 medium cucumbers (about 1 pound)*
> *1 tablespoon olive oil*
> *2 teaspoons champagne vinegar*
> *¼ teaspoon salt*
> *⅛ teaspoon freshly ground pepper*
> *2 tablespoons finely shredded mint leaves*

1. Peel the cucumbers and cut them lengthwise in half. With a spoon, scoop out the seeds if there are any. Cut the cucumbers crosswise into thin slices.

2. In a medium bowl, toss the cucumber slices with the olive oil, vinegar, salt and pepper. Let marinate for about 30 minutes, tossing occasionally.

3. Mix in the mint just before serving. If it is added earlier, it may darken.

— *Cucumber Barquettes Filled with Tapenade* —

In this "white" tapenade, a French country standard, water-packed tuna stands in for black olives. Try filling tomato halves as well as cucumbers for an even greater visual appeal, or use the tapenade as a zesty Mediterranean "tuna salad" in a sandwich. For added color, I like to garnish these with a bright radicchio leaf or a few slices of tomato and lemon wedges.

4 SERVINGS   12% CALORIES FROM FAT   142 CALORIES PER SERVING

> *2 cans (6⅛ ounces each) water-packed tuna, drained*
> *2 garlic cloves, crushed through a press*
> *1 tablespoon capers, drained*
> *1 tin (2 ounce) anchovies, drained and rinsed*
> *¼ cup lemon juice*
> *1 tablespoon Dijon mustard*
> *¼ teaspoon freshly ground pepper*
> *1 tablespoon chopped parsley*
> *2 small kirby cucumbers or 1 medium cucumber, peeled*

1. Place the tuna, garlic, capers, anchovies, lemon juice, mustard and pepper in a food processor and blend until a paste is formed. Stir in the parsley by hand.

2. Cut the kirby cucumbers lengthwise in half. If using a medium cucumber, cut each half crosswise into 4 equal pieces. Remove the seeds from each cucumber half by hollowing it out with a small spoon.

3. Fill the cucumber halves with the tapenade, dividing evenly.

— *Poached Leeks with Plum Tomatoes and Dijon* — *Vinaigrette*

Leeks figure prominently in French cuisine. Their mellow onion flavor serves as the base for many soups, stews and sauces. In this dish, the naturally slim leeks shine on their own. At only 120 calories per serving, you can add another 100 to sop up the delicious dressing with a chunk of crusty bread.

4 SERVINGS   29% CALORIES FROM FAT   122 CALORIES PER SERVING

> *8 small leeks (1 inch in diameter)*
> *1 can (14½ ounces) reduced-sodium chicken broth*
> *½ teaspoon coriander seeds*
> *1 lemon, sliced into thin rounds*
> *¼ teaspoon freshly ground pepper*
> *½ recipe Dijon Vinaigrette (page 36)*
> *2 plum tomatoes, cut into 8 wedges each*
> *1 tablespoon chopped parsley*

1. Trim the roots from the base of the leeks and cut off the very tops, but leave 6 inches of the green. Clean the leeks by splitting them down the middle with a large knife without cutting all the way through. (The white base should be split open like a book.) Dislodge all of the sand caught in the layers under cold running water. Tie the leek bottoms back together with white kitchen string.

2. In a high-sided medium skillet or wide saucepan, combine the chicken broth, coriander seeds, lemon slices and pepper. Bring to a boil, reduce the heat and simmer 5 minutes.

3. Add the leeks to the broth and cook over medium heat for 10 to 12 minutes, or until the white base of the leeks is tender when pierced with the tip of a knife. Remove the leeks with a slotted spoon and drain on a paper towel. Remove the strings.

4. Arrange the leeks on a small platter and while they are still warm pour the vinaigrette over them.

5. To serve, arrange the tomato wedges around the leeks and garnish with the chopped parsley. Spoon about ½ tablespoon dressing over each serving. Serve warm or at room temperature.

Eggplant Caviar

In this version of "poor man's caviar," or Provençal caviar, not a drop of oil is used. Instead, flavor is achieved by roasting the eggplants until they are soft and slightly smokey. Serve as a dip for crudités, or as a spread on thinly sliced bread or crackers, or with the Garlic Chapons that follow.

8 Servings   3% Calories from fat   28 Calories per serving

> *2 medium eggplants, about 1 pound each*
> *¼ cup lemon juice*
> *4 garlic cloves, crushed through a press*
> *6 to 12 drops of Tabasco, to taste*
> *½ teaspoon salt*
> *¼ teaspoon freshly ground pepper*

1. Preheat the oven to 400° F. Wrap each eggplant individually in aluminum foil and place on a baking sheet. Roast 1 hour, or until very soft. Unwrap carefully and let the eggplants cool down before handling.

2. Scrape the softened eggplant from the skins and place in a food processor or blender. Add the lemon juice, garlic, Tabasco, salt and pepper. Puree until completely smooth. Transfer to a serving bowl.

3. Cover and refrigerate for at least 2 hours, or until well chilled. Season with additional salt and pepper to taste. Serve the eggplant caviar very cold.

Garlic Chapons

4 Servings   27% Calories from fat   40 Calories per serving

> *1 teaspoon olive oil*
> *4 slices of crusty Italian or French bread, cut ½ inch thick*
> *2 garlic cloves, cut in half*

1. Preheat the oven to 400° F. Brush a 9-inch square baking dish with the olive oil.

2. Arrange the bread slices in the dish in a single layer. Bake the bread about 10 minutes, or until golden and crispy.

3. Rub the top side of the bread slices with the cut garlic cloves. Cut each slice of bread into 3 × ½-inch strips.

Pickled Red Onions

Raspberry vinegar tenderizes and sweetens the onions and turns them a lovely pink color. These delicate threads of onion can provide a piquant accent as part of a crudité plate or as a garnish on salads, sandwiches, meats or fish.

8 SERVINGS   2% CALORIES FROM FAT   24 CALORIES PER SERVING

2 large red onions (1 pound), peeled
3 tablespoons raspberry vinegar
1 teaspoon sugar

1. Cut the onions lengthwise in half and slice them into paper-thin half rounds using a mandoline or a food processor with a thin slicing blade attachment.

2. In a medium bowl, toss the onion slices with the raspberry vinegar and sugar until well coated.

3. Cover the bowl with plastic wrap and let the onions marinate in the refrigerator for at least 4 hours before serving.

Marinated Lentils

High in protein and low in fat, lentils are highly nourishing as well as satisfying. Serve as a light luncheon salad or as an accompaniment to grilled meat or fish. The cooked lentil base also makes an excellent soup: After cooking, divide the lentils in half. Puree one half and add it back to the remaining half. Add some reduced-sodium chicken broth if the soup is too thick and adjust the seasonings before reheating.

5 SERVINGS 28% CALORIES FROM FAT 200 CALORIES PER SERVING

> *1 cup lentils, rinsed and picked over to remove any grit*
> *1 can (14½ ounces) reduced-sodium chicken broth*
> *1 small carrot, finely chopped*
> *1 small onion, finely chopped*
> *¼ teaspoon dried thyme leaves*
> *1 bay leaf*
> *1 sprig of parsley plus 1 tablespoon chopped parsley*
> *¼ teaspoon salt*
> *⅛ teaspoon freshly ground pepper*
> *Dijon Vinaigrette (page 36)*
> *1 medium shallot, finely chopped*
> *8 leaves of butter lettuce, rinsed and dried*
> *1 tablespoon chopped chives*

1. Place the lentils, chicken broth, carrot, onion, thyme, bay leaf, parsley sprig, salt and pepper in a medium saucepan. Add 1 cup of water and bring to a boil. Reduce the heat to medium and simmer, uncovered, 30 to 45 minutes, or until the lentils are tender. (Some lentils cook faster than others.)

2. Drain the lentils and transfer to a medium bowl. Remove and discard the bay leaf and parsley sprig. Add the Dijon dressing, shallot and chopped parsley and toss until well combined. Cover and marinate the lentils in the refrigerator at least 2 hours or overnight.

3. Serve the lentils chilled or at room temperature, mounded on the butter lettuce leaves and garnished with the chopped chives.

Mixed Wild Mushroom and Field Mushroom Salad

Mushrooms are one of the tastiest and lightest ingredients available to the home cook. They contain no fat and very few calories. In preparing this salad remember—the more the merrier. Try to find a variety of mushrooms. The key here is in the contrast of flavors and textures. Meaty, tender cooked mushrooms are juxtaposed with crunchy raw ones. The effect is paradise for mushroom lovers—a veritable guilt-free mushroom feast!

4 Servings   60% Calories from fat   146 Calories per serving

> *1 pound mushrooms: shiitake, portobello, chanterelle, morel and/or*
> *oyster mushrooms, cleaned and cut into 1-inch pieces*
> *3 tablespoons extra virgin olive oil*
> *1 tablespoon reduced-sodium chicken broth*
> *1 tablespoon finely chopped garlic*
> *1/4 teaspoon salt*
> *1/8 teaspoon freshly ground pepper*
> *1/4 cup lemon juice*
> *1/4 pound fresh white mushrooms, cleaned and thinly sliced*
> *1 package (4 ounces) enoki mushrooms, cleaned*
> *12 sprigs of parsley*
> *1 lemon, cut into 8 wedges*

1. Preheat the oven to 400° F. In a small nonstick baking dish, toss the mushroom pieces with 1 tablespoon of the olive oil, the chicken broth and the garlic. Season with half the salt and pepper. Cover the dish tightly with a sheet of aluminum foil. Place in the oven and roast 15 to 20 minutes, or until the mushrooms are tender.

2. In a medium bowl, whisk together the remaining 2 tablespoons olive oil with the lemon juice and the remaining salt and pepper. Add the sliced raw mushrooms and the enoki mushrooms and stir until well mixed.

3. Arrange the parsley sprigs on a large plate and mound the warm cooked mushrooms in the center. Sprinkle the raw dressed mushrooms over the entire plate. Garnish with the lemon wedges.

Roasted Red Peppers Marinated with Capers, Olives and Anchovies

Here is a simple, light hors d'oeuvre that is more assembled than cooked. If time is of the essence, well-drained, jarred roasted red pepper strips can be substituted for the homemade ones suggested below.

4 SERVINGS   60% CALORIES FROM FAT   100 CALORIES PER SERVING

Roasted Red Peppers (recipe follows)
8 anchovy fillets, drained and rinsed
1 tablespoon capers, drained and rinsed
12 Mediterranean-style or other oil-cured black olives
1 tablespoon extra virgin olive oil
1 tablespoon lemon juice

Arrange the roasted pepper strips on a large plate like the spokes of a wheel. Place the anchovy fillets in between some of the spokes and sprinkle the capers and olives on top. Drizzle the extra virgin olive oil and lemon juice over all before serving.

Roasted Red Peppers

This technique for "roasting" peppers produces beautiful results. The red pepper skins peel off effortlessly, exposing fillets of luscious red pepper flesh. Since no oil is used in the process, these red peppers are about as low in calories as one can get.

4 SERVINGS   9% CALORIES FROM FAT   28 CALORIES PER SERVING

4 medium red bell peppers (about 1 pound)
½ cup reduced-sodium chicken broth

1. Preheat the oven to 400° F. Trim the top and bottom off each pepper and cut in half. Remove the seeds and inner white membranes, or ribs.

2. Line a small baking pan with a sheet of foil, leaving plenty of overlap. Arrange the peppers cut side-down on the foil in a single layer. Pour the chicken broth over all and bring the edges of foil together. Crimp to seal.

3. Bake 1 hour, or until the peppers are soft and the skin peels off easily. Let the peppers remain wrapped in the foil until they are cool enough to handle.

4. Peel off the skins with your fingers or with a small paring knife. Cut the peppers into 1-inch-thick strips.

Tomatoes Persillade

Vine-ripened summer tomatoes need very little in the way of enhancement. I find a splash of extra virgin olive oil, good vinegar and a touch of garlic and fresh herbs are all that's necessary to achieve perfection. If good ripe tomatoes are unavailable, try cherry tomatoes instead. They are usually quite reliable throughout the year.

4 SERVINGS   50% CALORIES FROM FAT   65 CALORIES PER SERVING

> *4 large ripe tomatoes (1½ pounds)*
> *1 tablespoon extra virgin olive oil*
> *2 teaspoons red wine vinegar*
> *1 teaspoon minced garlic*
> *2 tablespoons chopped parsley*
> *Salt and freshly ground pepper*

1. Remove the stem end from each tomato and slice into ¼-inch-thick rounds. Arrange the tomato slices, overlapping each other, on a serving plate.

2. Pour the olive oil and vinegar evenly over the tomatoes and sprinkle on the garlic and parsley. Season with salt and pepper to taste. Serve at room temperature.

Marinated Potato and Onion Salad

One taste of this thoroughly French potato salad and you'll swear it must be sinfully high in calories. But it's not. The secret lies in using some of the starchy potato cooking liquid to give the dressing body without adding fat.

5 SERVINGS   30% CALORIES FROM FAT   172 CALORIES PER SERVING

> 8 medium red potatoes (1½ pounds), scrubbed and cut into ¼-inch slices
> 3 tablespoons potato cooking water (see Step 1)
> Dijon Vinaigrette (recipe follows)
> ½ cup finely diced red onion
> ½ cup thinly sliced scallions
> 2 tablespoons chopped parsley
> ½ teaspoon salt
> ¼ teaspoon freshly ground pepper

1. In a medium saucepan, place the potatoes in enough cold water to cover. Bring to a boil, reduce the heat to medium and cook 5 to 8 minutes, or until tender but not mushy. Spoon 3 tablespoons of the cooking water into a medium bowl. Drain the potatoes and add to the bowl.

2. Add the vinaigrette, red onion, scallions, parsley, salt and pepper to the warm potatoes and toss gently to mix. Let marinate 2 hours before serving.

Dijon Vinaigrette

MAKES ½ CUP   32 CALORIES PER TABLESPOON   96% CALORIES FROM FAT

> 2 teaspoons Dijon mustard
> 2 tablespoons red wine vinegar
> 2 tablespoons olive oil
> ¼ cup water
> ¼ teaspoon salt
> ⅛ teaspoon freshly ground pepper

In a small bowl, or in a food processor, combine the mustard, vinegar, olive oil, water, salt and pepper. Whisk or blend until smooth.

Provençal Marinated Vegetable Sandwich

This snack was one of my childhood favorites. We often packed these stuffed buns for our *goûter* ("snack"), to be enjoyed during a winding drive up the back hills of Provence. It is essential that this sandwich marinate for at least 2 hours to allow the juices to penetrate the bread.

8 SERVINGS   27% CALORIES FROM FAT   179 CALORIES PER SERVING

Dijon Vinaigrette (page 36)
1 garlic clove, crushed through a press
1 tablespoon capers, drained
1 tin (2 ounces) anchovy fillets, drained, rinsed and chopped
1 medium green bell pepper, finely diced
½ medium red onion, finely diced
6 radishes, thinly sliced
1 small (4 ounces) cucumber, peeled, seeded and thinly sliced
2 celery ribs, thinly sliced
1 medium tomato, coarsely chopped
1 tablespoon chopped parsley
1 long crusty loaf of country bread (1½ pounds)

1. In a large bowl, combine the Dijon vinaigrette with the garlic, capers, anchovies, green pepper, red onion, radishes, cucumber, celery, tomato and parsley. Toss until well mixed.

2. Slice off about the top fourth of the loaf of bread; remove the "cap" and set aside. Pull out the soft center down the length of the loaf, leaving a ½-inch-thick layer of bread inside the crust.

3. Stuff the vegetable mixture inside the loaf. Press down on the vegetables to make them fit. Replace the "cap" on top. Wrap the bread tightly in plastic wrap and refrigerate 2 to 4 hours.

4. To serve, cut the loaf crosswise into 6 sandwiches.

Wild Mushroom Ragout Tartines

The robust flavor of mushrooms is thoroughly satisfying atop crusty, garlic-rubbed bread. In Italy these would be called crostini, in France they are known as *croûtes* or *tartines*. Try pairing these with salad for a light entree. The mushroom ragout is delicious on its own as a vegetable, tossed with pasta or as a base for soup.

4 SERVINGS   28% CALORIES FROM FAT   147 CALORIES PER SERVING

> *4 slices of French or Italian bread, cut ½ inch thick*
> *1 teaspoon chopped garlic plus 1 garlic clove, cut in half*
> *1 teaspoon olive oil*
> *½ pound shiitake mushrooms, cleaned and sliced*
> *½ pound oyster mushrooms, cleaned and sliced*
> *½ pound fresh white button or brown cremini mushrooms, cleaned, trimmed and sliced*
> *¼ teaspoon salt*
> *⅛ teaspoon freshly ground pepper*
> *2 tablespoons port*
> *1 tablespoon chopped parsley*
> *¼ cup shredded Gruyère cheese*

1. Toast the bread slices or grill them under the broiler until lightly browned, 1 to 2 minutes. Rub the tops with the cut garlic. Set the *tartines* aside.

2. Brush the olive oil over the bottom of a large nonstick skillet. Add the mushrooms, chopped garlic, salt and pepper and cook over medium heat, stirring often, until the mushrooms give off their liquid, about 5 minutes.

3. Add the port and boil over high heat until the liquid is reduced and syrupy. Toss in the parsley and remove the mushroom ragout from the heat.

4. Preheat the boiler. Divide the mushroom ragout among the 4 slices of garlic bread. Cut each slice diagonally in half.

5. Arrange the pieces on a cookie sheet and sprinkle the Gruyère evenly over the tops. Broil about 4 inches from the heat about 3 minutes, until the cheese just begins to bubble. Serve at once.

Salmon Rillettes

Traditionally rillettes are made with duck, goose or pork that is slow cooked in its own fat until the meat is totally soft. The mixture is then cooled off and when the fat is solid, it is enjoyed as a spread on bread. Recently, French cooks have applied the same techniques with great success to flavorful fish such as salmon.

In this lightened version, I have reduced the fat by substituting nonfat cream cheese for butter. Enjoy this spread on toasted bread or as a light entree with some marinated green beans, Roasted Red Peppers (page 34) and Pickled Red Onions (page 31).

4 SERVINGS   22% CALORIES FROM FAT   194 CALORIES PER SERVING

1/2 pound boneless salmon fillet, skinned and cut into 1-inch chunks
1/2 cup white vermouth or dry white wine
2 tablespoons finely chopped shallots
1/4 pound thinly sliced smoked salmon, cut into 1/4-inch dice
8 ounces nonfat whipped cream cheese
3 tablespoons lemon juice
Salt and freshly ground pepper

1. Place the salmon fillet, vermouth and shallots in a medium nonreactive skillet. Bring to a boil and cook over high heat until the liquid is reduced to a syrup, 5 to 8 minutes. Pour the contents of the skillet into a shallow bowl and let cool.

2. Scrape the cooled cooked salmon with its shallots and syrup into a food processor. Add the smoked salmon, cream cheese and lemon juice. Mix well, pulsing the machine on and off, until a chunky paste is obtained. Season with salt and pepper to taste.

3. Scrape the salmon rillettes into a small bowl. Cover with plastic wrap and refrigerate 4 to 6 hours, or until well chilled and set enough to spread.

Citrus "Cooked" Salmon on a Bed of Fresh Herbs

Sparkling fresh salmon fillets and fresh squeezed lemon juice are a must for this French version of "seviche." Serve this elegant dish as a first course or as a light luncheon with a slice of Toasted Garlic Bread (page 57).

4 SERVINGS   52% CALORIES FROM FAT   155 CALORIES PER SERVING

> *12 ounces salmon fillet, boned and skinned*
> *1 cup lemon juice*
> *1 teaspoon ground coriander*
> *½ teaspoon salt*
> *¼ teaspoon freshly ground pepper*
> *12 sprigs of assorted fresh herbs, such as basil, marjoram, thyme, mint,*
>   *chervil or parsley*
> *1 tablespoon extra virgin olive oil*

1. Slice the salmon by holding a sharp knife almost horizontally while cutting slices as thinly as possible.

2. Coat the bottom of a flat glass dish with half of the lemon juice. Sprinkle with half of the coriander, salt and pepper.

3. Lay all of the fish slices in one even layer in the dish. Pour the remaining lemon juice over the fish and sprinkle with the remaining seasonings.

4. Let marinate for 10 minutes, then turn each piece over and marinate 5 minutes for medium-rare and up to 20 minutes longer for well done.

5. To serve, arrange some of the herbs on a plate so that their stems face the center. Arrange the fish slices in the center. Moisten with some of the marinade and drizzle the extra virgin olive oil over the fish.

Oysters with 3 Mignonette Sauces

Fresh oysters are a French ritual. Serve them with thin slices of black bread, lemon wedges and, of course, plenty of mignonette sauce. I think the reason oysters are considered an aphrodisiac is that they are so naturally low in calories and light that one never feels overly full after slurping down a few. Oysters are a sensuous treat—enjoy them with someone you love.

8 Servings   25% Calories from fat   38 Calories per serving

24 freshly shucked oysters

Mignonette #1:
2 tablespoons minced shallots
¼ cup red wine vinegar
⅛ teaspoon cracked black pepper

Mignonette #2:
2 tablespoons minced shallots
¼ cup champagne vinegar
1 teaspoon chopped fresh tarragon leaves or parsley
⅛ teaspoon cracked black pepper

Mignonette #3:
2 tablespoons minced shallots
¼ cup cider vinegar
1 teaspoon chopped parsley
1 teaspoon chopped chives
⅛ teaspoon cracked black pepper

1. Present the oysters on a bed of seaweed or cracked ice.

2. Combine the ingredients for each mignonette sauce in 3 separate small bowls and serve with the oysters.

Chapter Two

SOUPS

The French are connoisseurs of soup. Famous chefs and humble home cooks alike are judged on the basis of how flavorful their soups are. The evening meal in France is even called *le souper,* which is where our word for supper comes from. The name came about because this meal was always centered around soup. Traditionally, the French eat their main meal—*le dejeuner*—in the middle of the day. Therefore, the evening meal is always a light repast, which usually consists of some salad based on leftovers from lunch, a steaming bowl of soup and some cheese or fruit for dessert.

Healthy and soup are almost synonymous to the French. For in their evening bowl of *potage,* or vegetable soup, they want to be comforted and restored, to savor the purity of the fresh ingredients within.

There are two categories of soup in French cooking: the light vegetable-based *potages* and the more substantial meals in a bowl, such as *bouillabaisse.* For our purposes, this chapter will focus on the light fresh vegetable-based soups that are eaten nightly all over the French countryside. The main-course soups, or stews, can be found elsewhere.

All of the soups in this chapter are prepared with a minimum of fat—never more than 1 tablespoon for a whole potful—and they are enriched with nonfat milk instead of cream. Where appropriate, as in many of the creamy pureed soups, body is derived from potatoes. Because most of us simply don't have the time to prepare long-simmered homemade stock, I call for reduced-sodium chicken broth. Vegetarians can substitute canned vegetable stock and reduce the amount of salt used in seasoning.

Several of these soups call for foil "sautéing" the vegetables. A sheet of aluminum foil is pressed right on top of the vegetables as they cook in a tablespoon or less of oil. This is a crucial step in low-calorie soup and stew making. Vegetables cooked in this way release their natural sugars and make a very flavorful soup, while requiring only a small amount of fat in which to cook. For more information on foil "sautéing," refer to page 17.

White Winter Root Vegetable Soup

Winter root vegetables such as turnips, parsnips, and celery root are often overlooked, which is unfortunate because these vegetables are absolutely delicious and naturally low in calories. They are often the "surprise" ingredient in the new low-fat sauces featured at fancy restaurants.

6 Servings   26% Calories from fat   120 Calories per serving

> 1 tablespoon olive oil
> 2 medium onions, cut into 1-inch chunks
> 1 large parsnip, peeled and cut into 1-inch chunks
> 2 medium leeks (white part only), split, well cleaned and cut into
>   1-inch pieces
> 1 large turnip, peeled and cut into 1-inch chunks
> 1 medium celery root (celeriac), peeled and cut into 1-inch chunks
> 3 cans (14½ ounces each) reduced-sodium chicken broth
> 1 cup nonfat milk
> Salt and freshly ground pepper

1. In a large heavy pot, heat the olive oil and add the onions and parsnip. Press a sheet of aluminum foil right down on top of the vegetables. Cook over medium heat, stirring once or twice, until the onions are tender, about 5 minutes. Remove the foil.

2. Add the leeks, turnip, celery root, chicken broth and enough water to just cover the vegetables, about 1 cup. Bring to a boil, reduce the heat and simmer, partially covered, 20 to 25 minutes, or until all the vegetables are tender.

3. In a food processor or blender, in batches if necessary, puree the soup until smooth. Return to the pot and stir in the milk until blended. Season with salt and pepper to taste. (The soup can be made up to a day in advance.) Reheat until hot before serving.

Creamy Carrot Soup

There's no cream here, just a smooth puree of melting carrots smoothed out with some nonfat milk. In France, this is called *soupe de Crécy*, after the village of Crécy, which is famous for growing the best carrots in the country. Since the flavor of the vegetable dominates, use fresh bunched carrots whenever they are available.

4 SERVINGS   26% CALORIES FROM FAT   156 CALORIES PER SERVING

> *1 tablespoon olive oil*
> *1 medium onion, chopped*
> *1 large baking potato (about ½ pound), peeled and cut into 1-inch chunks*
> *1 pound carrots, peeled and cut into 1-inch pieces*
> *2 cans (14½ ounces each) reduced-sodium chicken broth*
> *1 cup nonfat milk*
> *Salt and freshly ground pepper*

1. In a large saucepan, heat the olive oil. Add the onion, cover and cook over medium heat 2 minutes. Uncover and cook, stirring occasionally, until the onion is soft and lightly colored, about 3 minutes longer.

2. Add the potato, carrots and chicken broth. Bring to a boil, reduce the heat and simmer, partially covered, 30 minutes.

3. Puree the soup in a food processor or blender. Return to the pot and stir in the milk until blended. Season with salt and pepper to taste. Reheat until hot before serving.

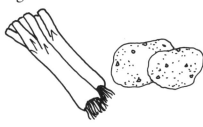

Chilled Cucumber Soup

On a hot summer day in Provence, this light soup was always a refreshing treat.

4 SERVINGS   30% CALORIES FROM FAT   150 CALORIES PER SERVING

> 1 tablespoon olive oil
> 1 medium onion, chopped
> 1 large baking potato (about ½ pound), peeled and cut into 1-inch
>   pieces
> 1 can (14½ ounces) reduced-sodium chicken broth
> 3 large cucumbers (1½ pounds), peeled, seeded and chopped
> 1 cup nonfat plain yogurt
> Salt and freshly ground pepper
> ¼ cup low-fat sour cream
> 1 tablespoon chopped chives

1. In a large pot, heat the olive oil. Add the onion, cover and cook over medium heat 2 minutes. Uncover and cook, stirring occasionally, until soft and lightly colored, 3 to 5 minutes longer.

2. Add the potato and chicken broth and bring to a boil. Reduce the heat and simmer 15 to 20 minutes, or until the potato is tender.

3. In a food processor or blender, in batches if necessary, puree the cucumbers with the soup until smooth. Blend in the yogurt. Season with salt and pepper to taste. Transfer to a covered container and refrigerate at least 3 hours, or until thoroughly chilled.

4. Serve cold with 1 tablespoon sour cream and ¾ teaspoon chives garnishing each bowl.

Chilled Tomato Soup with Mint, Herbed Croutons and Feta Cheese

Corsican feta, known as "French" feta, is less salty than Greek feta. Feta is a naturally low-fat cheese that adds zip to soup, salads, pasta and vegetables. In this soup, it offsets the natural sweetness of the tomatoes and onions.

4 TO 6 SERVINGS   42% CALORIES FROM FAT   155 CALORIES PER SERVING

> *1 tablespoon extra virgin olive oil*
> *1 medium onion, chopped*
> *2 garlic cloves, finely chopped*
> *2 cans (14 ounces each) low-salt chopped tomatoes, juices reserved*
> *1 can (14½ ounces) reduced-sodium chicken broth*
> *Salt and freshly ground pepper*
> *2 tablespoons finely shredded mint*
> *Herbed Croutons (recipe follows)*
> *2 ounces feta cheese, preferably French, crumbled (about ½ cup)*

1. In a medium nonreactive saucepan, heat the olive oil. Add the onion, cover and cook over medium heat 2 minutes. Uncover and cook, stirring occasionally, until soft and lightly colored, about 3 minutes longer.

2. Add the garlic, tomatoes and chicken broth and simmer over medium heat 10 minutes.

3. Transfer the soup to a food processor or blender and puree until smooth. Season with salt and pepper to taste. Cover and refrigerate at least 3 hours, or until cold.

4. Serve the tomato soup well chilled, garnished with the mint, croutons and feta cheese.

Herbed Croutons

4 SERVINGS   27% CALORIES FROM FAT   67 CALORIES PER SERVING

1 teaspoon olive oil
4 slices (½-inch) of stale French or Italian bread, cut into ½-inch dice
1 tablespoon grated Parmesan cheese
1 tablespoon chopped parsley
¼ teaspoon freshly ground pepper

1. Preheat the oven to 400° F. Brush the olive oil over a small baking sheet.

2. Spread out the bread pieces on the oiled baking sheet in a single layer. Bake about 10 minutes, or until golden and crispy.

3. In a medium bowl, combine the Parmesan cheese, parsley and pepper. Add the warm croutons to the mixture and toss to coat. Then spread back out on the baking sheet to cool.

Leek and Potato Soup

There's something magical about the way French country cooking transforms humble ingredients, such as leeks and potatoes, into such a fabulous soup. For a chunky effect, puree only half of the vegetables.

6 SERVINGS   6% CALORIES FROM FAT   148 CALORIES PER SERVING

4 large leeks (white and tender green), split, well cleaned and thickly sliced
4 large baking potatoes (about 2 pounds), peeled and cut into 1-inch chunks
2 cans (14½ ounces each) reduced-sodium chicken broth
1 cup nonfat milk
Salt and freshly ground pepper

1. In a large saucepan, combine the leeks, potatoes, chicken broth and 3 cups of water. Bring to a boil, lower the heat and simmer 20 to 25 minutes, or until the potatoes are very soft.

2. Puree the soup in a food processor or blender until smooth. Return to the pan and stir in the milk until blended. Season with salt and pepper to taste. Reheat until hot before serving or cover and refrigerate until chilled and serve cold.

Gratinéed Onion Soup

Onion soup gratinée is perhaps the best-known of all French soups in America. This is the way we always prepared it at home. The soup attains its intense onion flavor through the long, slow cooking process of softening and coloring, or caramelizing, the onions. Therefore, the step involving cooking down the onions until they are dark golden in color is crucial.

4 SERVINGS   24% CALORIES FROM FAT   200 CALORIES PER SERVING

> 2 teaspoons olive oil
> 1¾ pounds onions, thinly sliced
> 2 teaspoons finely chopped garlic
> 1 bay leaf
> 2 tablespoons flour
> 1 can (14½ ounces) reduced-sodium chicken broth
> Salt and freshly ground pepper
> Toasted Garlic Bread (recipe follows)
> 2 tablespoons grated Parmesan cheese
> 2 tablespoons shredded Gruyère cheese

1. In a large nonstick pot, heat the olive oil and add the onions, garlic and bay leaf. Press a sheet of aluminum foil right down on top of the onions. Cook over medium heat, stirring occasionally, until the onions are soft and dark golden in color, 20 to 30 minutes. Remove the foil, scraping any onions that stick to it back into the pot.

2. Sprinkle the flour over the onions and cook, stirring, 1 minute. Add the chicken broth and 2 cups of water. Bring to a boil, reduce the heat to medium-low, partially cover and simmer 30 minutes.

3. Puree half of the soup in a blender or food processor; return to the pot. Season with salt and pepper to taste. (The soup can be made to this point up to 2 days in advance. Cover and refrigerate.)

4. To serve, preheat the broiler. Reheat the onion soup, if necessary. Place 1 slice of garlic toast in the bottom of each of 4 flameproof soup bowls. Ladle the onion soup over the bread. Sprinkle each serving with ½ tablespoon each of Parmesan and Gruyère cheese. Broil about 4 inches from the heat 2 to 3 minutes, until the cheeses are melted.

Toasted Garlic Bread

Tartines à la frotte, as these are called in French, loosely translates as "rubbed bread." This is the French version of the Italian *bruschetta,* garlic-rubbed bread, prepared here without the olive oil. A good-quality crusty country loaf is essential to the flavor of *la frotte.*

4 SERVINGS   9% CALORIES FROM FAT   52 CALORIES PER SERVING

> *4 slices of good, crusty French or Italian bread, cut ½ inch thick*
> *1 large garlic clove, peeled*

1. Preheat the oven to 400° F.

2. Place the bread on a cookie sheet and toast in the oven 5 to 10 minutes, or until it begins to turn golden brown.

3. While the toasted bread slices are still warm, rub them on top with a raw garlic clove.

Variation:

Prepare the Garlic Toasts as described above, but instead of rubbing them with the raw garlic, spread 1 tablespoon Sweet Garlic Puree (page 133) over each slice.

Soupe au Pistou

This French provincial vegetable soup with basil and garlic is a complete meal in itself. Serve with slices of Toasted Garlic Bread (preceding recipe).

6 Servings   30% Calories from fat   199 Calories per serving

> 1 tablespoon olive oil
> 2 medium onions, cut into ½-inch dice
> 2 medium carrots, peeled and cut into ½-inch dice
> 2 medium zucchini, cut into ½-inch dice
> ¼ pound green beans, trimmed and cut into 1-inch pieces
> 1 can (14 ounces) low-salt chopped tomatoes, drained
> 6 garlic cloves, minced
> ½ pound potatoes, peeled and cut into ¾-inch chunks
> 2 cans (14½ ounces each) reduced-sodium chicken broth
> 1 cup chick peas, preferably low-salt, rinsed and drained
> Salt and freshly ground pepper
> Pistou (recipe follows)
> 2 tablespoons grated Parmesan cheese

1. In a large pot, heat the olive olive and add the onions and carrots. Press a sheet of aluminum foil right down on top of the vegetables. Cook over medium heat, stirring once or twice, until the onions are golden and the carrots are tender, 7 to 10 minutes. Remove the foil.

2. Add the zucchini, green beans, tomatoes, garlic, potatoes, chicken broth and 2 cups of water. Bring to a boil, reduce the heat to medium and simmer, partially covered, 20 minutes.

3. Add the chick peas and cook 5 minutes longer. Season the soup with salt and pepper to taste.

4. To serve, ladle the hot soup into bowls. Spoon about 2 tablespoons pistou and 1 teaspoon grated cheese on top of each.

Pistou

Pistou is French country cooking's answer to Italian *pesto*. Serve this lightened, low-calorie version as a condiment in soups or with grilled or poached meats or fish, or double the recipe and toss with pasta.

MAKES ABOUT ⅔ CUP   66% CALORIES FROM FAT   18 CALORIES PER TABLESPOON

> *1 cup packed basil leaves*
> *1 tablespoon olive oil*
> *2 garlic cloves, crushed through a press*
> *½ cup reduced-sodium chicken broth*
> *Salt and freshly ground pepper*

In a blender or food processor, combine the basil leaves with the olive oil, garlic and chicken broth. Puree until smooth. Season with salt and pepper to taste.

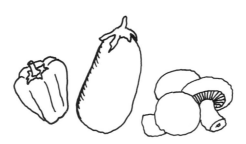

Sweet Pea, Lettuce and Mint Soup

For a refreshing change of pace, try this light lettuce, pea and mint soup. Frozen peas, picked at peak sweetness, work best here, which makes the soup as convenient as it is delicious. For a thicker soup, try pureeing half of the vegetables and mixing them back into the rest.

6 SERVINGS   17% CALORIES FROM FAT   174 CALORIES PER SERVING

1 tablespoon olive oil
1 medium onion, finely diced
1 small bay leaf
Pinch of thyme
1 pound red potatoes, peeled and cut into ½-inch dice
1 can (14½ ounces) reduced-sodium chicken broth
2 packages (10 ounces each) frozen peas, thawed and drained
1 large head of Boston or bibb lettuce (1 pound), thinly sliced
Salt and freshly ground pepper
1 tablespoon shredded fresh mint

1. In a large saucepan, heat the olive oil. Add the onion, cover and cook over medium heat 2 minutes. Uncover and cook, stirring occasionally, until the onion is tender and lightly colored, 3 to 5 minutes.

2. Add the bay leaf, thyme, potatoes, chicken broth and 2 cups of water. Bring to a boil, reduce the heat and simmer 15 minutes.

3. Add the peas and lettuce and simmer 5 minutes longer. Season with salt and pepper to taste. Garnish with the mint just before serving.

Puree of Garden Vegetable Soup

This *potage de la jardinière*, as it's called in French, is another simple country soup, similar to *potage santé*. Pureeing the vegetables adds an extra dimension of flavor and texture to this basic formula, creating a creaminess without any added calories or fat.

6 SERVINGS   23% CALORIES FROM FAT   121 CALORIES PER SERVING

> 1 tablespoon olive oil
> 2 medium onions, coarsely chopped
> 2 large carrots, peeled and coarsely chopped
> 1 medium turnip, peeled and coarsely chopped
> 1 large parsnip, peeled and coarsely chopped
> 1 large potato, peeled and coarsely chopped
> 1 large leek (white and tender green), split, well cleaned and cut into
>   1-inch slices
> 2 cans (14½ ounces each) reduced-sodium chicken broth
> 1 cup nonfat milk
> Salt and freshly ground pepper

1. In a large saucepan, heat the olive oil and add the onions and carrots. Press a sheet of aluminum foil right down on top of the vegetables. Cook over medium heat, stirring once or twice, until the onions are lightly colored and the carrots are tender, 7 to 10 minutes.

2. Add the turnip, parsnip, potato, leek, chicken broth and 3 cups of water to the pot. Bring to a boil, reduce the heat and simmer 25 to 30 minutes, or until the vegetables are tender.

3. Transfer the vegetables and broth to a blender or food processor and puree until smooth. Return to the pan and stir in the milk until blended. Season with salt and pepper to taste. Reheat until hot before serving.

Chunky Vegetable "Potage Santé"

Potage santé means "health soup," which gives some idea of just how pure and simple this dish is. Chunks of vegetables are quickly cooked in broth until tender. The addition of sorrel or spinach at the last moment adds a really fresh taste as well as extra nutrition.

6 SERVINGS   9% CALORIES FROM FAT   91 CALORIES PER SERVING

> 2 large carrots, peeled and cut into 1-inch chunks
> 2 medium leeks (white and tender green parts), split, well rinsed and
>   cut into 1-inch pieces
> 1 large baking potato (about ¾ pound), peeled and cut into 1-inch
>   chunks
> 1 large turnip, peeled and cut into 1-inch chunks
> 1 large parsnip, peeled and cut into 1-inch chunks
> 2 cans (14½ ounces each) reduced-sodium chicken broth
> ½ pound sorrel or spinach leaves, cleaned and thinly sliced
> Salt and freshly ground pepper

1. In a small stockpot or large saucepan, combine the carrots, leeks, potato, turnip, parsnip, chicken broth and 3 cups of water. Bring to a boil over high heat. Reduce the heat and simmer 15 to 20 minutes, or until the vegetables are tender.

2. Stir in the sorrel. Season with salt and pepper to taste and serve piping hot.

Watercress, Potato and Onion Soup: Soupe à la Cressionière

The peppery flavor of watercress makes a delightfully tasty soup. Naturally low in calories, watercress is also a rich source of many vitamins and minerals.

4 SERVINGS   23% CALORIES FROM FAT   172 CALORIES PER SERVING

> 1 tablespoon olive oil
> 2 medium onions, coarsely chopped
> 2 large baking potatoes (1 pound total), cut into 1-inch chunks
> 2 large bunches of watercress, rinsed and coarsely chopped
> 2 cans (14½ ounces each) reduced-sodium chicken broth
> ½ cup nonfat milk
> Salt and freshly ground pepper

1. In a large saucepan, heat the olive oil. Add the onions, cover and cook over medium heat 2 minutes. Uncover and cook, stirring until softened and lightly colored, 3 to 5 minutes longer.

2. Add the potatoes, watercress and chicken broth. Bring to a boil, reduce the heat and simmer 15 to 20 minutes, or until the potatoes are tender.

3. Puree in a food processor or blender. Return to the pot and stir in the milk until blended. Season with salt and pepper to taste. Reheat until hot before serving.

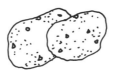

Zucchini and Rice Soup

Another exercise in simplicity, zucchini and rice soup is really quite delicious with a dollop of Pistou (page 53), or Red Pepper Coulis (page 96), or with 1 can (14 ounces) low-salt chopped tomatoes, drained, stirred in along with a sprinkling of Parmesan cheese on top.

6 SERVINGS   20% CALORIES FROM FAT   144 CALORIES PER SERVING

1 tablespoon olive oil
2 medium onions, cut into ½-inch dice
2 garlic cloves, finely chopped
1 pound zucchini, thinly sliced
2 cans (14½ ounces each) reduced-sodium chicken broth
2 cups cooked rice
Salt and freshly ground pepper
1 tablespoon chopped parsley
1 tablespoon finely shredded basil (or use 1 more tablespoon parsley)

1. In a large saucepan, heat the olive oil. Add the onions, cover and cook over medium heat 2 minutes. Uncover and cook, stirring occasionally until soft and translucent, 3 to 5 minutes.

2. Add the garlic, zucchini, chicken broth and 2 cups of water. Bring to a boil, reduce the heat and simmer 10 minutes, or until the zucchini are tender.

3. Add the rice and simmer 5 minutes longer. Season with salt and pepper to taste. Serve hot, garnished with the parsley and basil.

Chapter Three

SALADS
AND
COLD
ENTREES

Salad making in France is a veritable art, though it wasn't until 25 years ago that salads became really popular. The *nouvelle cuisine,* a culinary revolution on both sides of the Atlantic, called for lighter, fresher, healthier food, and suddenly everyone's eating habits began to change. There was an explosion of salads. While chefs were busy creating strange, exotic combinations, French home cooks took a more practical approach by using leftovers to create light, healthful entrees. Now, salads have become so ingrained in the French diet that they are as sacred as the evening bowl of soup. The French salad palette offers a myriad of possibilities. Even the basics are dizzying to choose from: a dozen different kinds of oils and as many vinegars, along with sweet greens, bitter greens and pungent greens: *frisée, roquette* (arugula), mesclun, watercress and endive, to name a few. I've developed the recipes in this book using only a few basic oils and vinegars (see "About the Ingredients," page 14), but the possibilities for creativity are endless, using cooked or raw vegetables, fish, meats, cheeses and nuts.

The salads in this chapter can be divided into three categories. Appetizer salads, which are light and simple, but have ample play of colors and textures—Beet, Endive, Watercress and Onion or Apple, Watercress, and Endive Salad with Roquefort Cheese and Roasted Walnut Dressing, for example. Composed salads, which are slightly more substantial and are designed to be served as a first course or a light lunch: Green Bean and Hazelnut Salad with Lemon Dijon Yogurt Dressing, Mesclun Salad with Roasted Chèvre and Smoked Fish Salad with Capers, Pickled Red Onions and Spinach, to name a few. And heartier salads, including Salade Niçoise, Warm Chicken Breast Salad with Sherry Shallot Dressing and Warm Roasted Salmon Salad with Mesclun, Potato, Onion and Bacon, which are really cold entrees, or main-course salads. Many of the composed and main-course salads can be served in smaller portions as an appetizer, or first course.

Included also are some very innovative and fabulous low-calorie French dressings that you'll want to use over and over again, such as Lemon-Garlic Vinaigrette, Lemon Dijon Yogurt Dressing, Sherry Shallot Dressing, Roasted Orange Thyme Vinaigrette, Lemon Honey-Date Dressing, Hot Bacon and Calvados Dressing, Champagne Cumin Vinaigrette, Raspberry Vinaigrette and Roasted Walnut Dressing. Made with a bare minimum of oil, these dressings rely more on low-calorie condiments, such as Dijon mustard, flavored vinegars, spices, garlic, shallots and fresh herbs. Vinaigrettes are given added body by replacing part of the oil with reduced-sodium chicken broth or yogurt.

All of these salads are an adventure in light, low-calorie eating. Use them as a guide for creating your own innovations with leftover cooked vegetables, fish or meat.

— *Asparagus, Endive and Orange Salad with* — *Raspberry Vinaigrette*

Raspberry vinaigrette is also very good with green beans, poached fish or chicken breasts. If a thicker dressing is desired, whip ¼ cup drained soft tofu in a food processor or blender and mix it into the dressing.

4 Servings   30% Calories from fat   104 Calories per serving

1¼ to 1½ pounds fresh asparagus, to yield 1 pound trimmed
3 navel oranges
2 Belgian endives, separated into leaves
1 tablespoon raspberry vinegar
1 teaspoon Dijon mustard
1 tablespoon olive oil
1 tablespoon finely chopped chives
⅛ teaspoon salt
⅛ teaspoon freshly ground pepper

1. Cut off the tough stems from the asparagus. Cut the asparagus crosswise on a slight diagonal into 1½-inch lengths. In a large saucepan of boiling water, cook the asparagus until just tender, 2 to 3 minutes. Drain into a colander, rinse briefly under cold running water and drain well. Transfer to a medium bowl.

2. With a small sharp knife, cut the peel off 2 of the oranges, removing all the bitter white pith. Cut down on either side of the membranes to release the segments. Add the orange segments and the Belgian endive leaves to the asparagus. Grate the zest from the remaining orange and set aside. Cut the orange in half and squeeze out the juice. Set aside ¼ cup. Reserve the remainder for another use.

3. In a blender or small food processor, combine the vinegar, reserved orange zest and juice, mustard and olive oil. Process until thoroughly emulsified. Stir in the chives and season the dressing with the salt and pepper.

4. Pour the dressing over the asparagus, orange and endive and toss well until coated. Divide among 4 plates and serve.

Apple, Watercress and Endive Salad with Roquefort Cheese and Roasted Walnut Dressing

Apples and Roquefort cheese along with walnut dressing jazz up this perennial French country favorite.

4 Servings   57% Calories from fat   194 Calories per serving

2 large bunches of watercress, tough stems removed
2 Belgian endives, separated into leaves
Roasted Walnut Dressing (page 63)
2 medium sweet red apples, thinly sliced
1 teaspoon lemon juice
2 ounces Roquefort or other blue-veined cheese, crumbled (about ½ cup)

1. In a medium mixing bowl, combine the watercress and endives. Add the walnut dressing and toss to mix. Divide the salad among 4 plates.

2. In the same mixing bowl, toss the apple slices with the lemon juice and arrange on top of the greens.

3. Sprinkle one-fourth of the Roquefort cheese over each salad and serve.

Arugula, Endive and Beets with Roasted Walnut Dressing

Arugula, known as *la roquette* in France, has a pleasant nutty, peppery flavor that is a perfect foil to crisp Belgian endives, sweet luscious beets and rich roasted walnut dressing. Arugula is increasingly common in the produce sections of supermarkets across America, and you should know that it grows easily—even in a flowerpot.

4 Servings   66% Calories from fat   107 Calories per serving

2 Belgian endives, separated into leaves
½ pound arugula, rinsed and drained

1 cup sliced cooked or canned beets
Roasted Walnut Dressing (recipe follows)

1. Arrange the endive leaves on a small round platter, with the points of the spears facing out.

2. In a medium bowl, combine the arugula and beets. Pour the walnut dressing over the vegetables and toss to coat. Mound the arugula and beets in the center of the platter and serve.

Roasted Walnut Dressing

In France, fragrant walnut oil is frequently used in salad dressing. While the oil is available here, it is quite costly and spoils quickly, so I devised this substitute, using Asian sesame oil and toasted walnuts to achieve the same effect. Roasted walnut dressing is especially delicious on steamed green beans.

MAKES ABOUT ½ CUP   42 CALORIES PER TABLESPOON   86% CALORIES FROM FAT

¼ cup walnuts
1 tablespoon Dijon mustard
1 tablespoon sherry wine vinegar
1 teaspoon Asian sesame oil
2 teaspoons olive oil
2 tablespoons reduced-sodium chicken broth
Salt and freshly ground pepper

1. Preheat the oven to 375° F. Spread out the nuts in a small baking dish and toast in the oven 5 to 7 minutes, or until fragrant and lightly browned. Immediately transfer to a small dish and let cool.

2. In a food processor or blender, combine 2 tablespoons of the toasted walnuts with the mustard, vinegar, sesame oil, olive oil and chicken broth. Blend until smooth. Season the dressing with salt and pepper to taste.

3. Chop the remaining walnuts. Transfer the dressing to a small bowl and stir in the chopped nuts.

— Beet, Endive, Watercress and Onion Salad — with Lemon-Garlic Vinaigrette

Belgian endives are very common in French cooking. Their refreshing zesty flavor adds a crisp touch to salads. Look for pale, white heads with tightly bunched leaves. This is a traditional holiday salad. Its beautiful greens and reds and attractive composition make it perfect for entertaining, either as a side salad or as a starter.

4 SERVINGS   36% CALORIES FROM FAT   82 CALORIES PER SERVING

> *Lemon-Garlic Vinaigrette (recipe follows)*
> *2 large bunches of watercress, tough stems removed*
> *1 can (16 ounces) sliced beets, drained*
> *2 Belgian endives, rinsed and separated into leaves*
> *½ cup very thinly sliced sweet onion, preferably red*

1. In a large bowl, combine half of the garlic vinaigrette with the watercress and beets. Toss well to coat.

2. Arrange the endive leaves on a round platter with the points of the spears facing out. Mound the watercress and beets in the center. Scatter the onion slices over the salad.

3. Pour the remaining vinaigrette over all and serve.

— Lemon-Garlic Vinaigrette —

If you have any Sweet Garlic Puree (page 133) on hand, stir a tablespoon of it into this dressing for an intense yet subtle boost of the garlic flavor.

MAKES ABOUT ⅓ CUP   88% CALORIES FROM FAT   28 CALORIES PER TABLESPOON

> *1 teaspoon Dijon mustard*
> *1 tablespoon red wine vinegar*
> *1 tablespoon lemon juice*
> *⅛ teaspoon salt*
> *⅛ teaspoon freshly ground pepper*

1 tablespoon olive oil
2 tablespoons water
1 garlic clove, crushed through a press
1 tablespoon chopped parsley
½ teaspoon grated lemon zest

In a small bowl, whisk together the mustard, vinegar, lemon juice, salt and pepper until well blended. Gradually whisk in the oil and water. Blend in the garlic, parsley and lemon zest.

— *Fresh Fennel, Orange and Olive Salad with* — *Gruyère Cheese*

On sweltering summer days in Provence, this light cooling salad was always a treat.

4 SERVINGS   52% CALORIES FROM FAT   155 CALORIES PER SERVING

1 large fennel bulb (about 1 pound)
2 large navel oranges, peeled and cut into thin rounds
¼ cup orange juice, preferably freshly squeezed
1 tablespoon lemon juice
1 tablespoon extra virgin olive oil
⅛ teaspoon salt
⅛ teaspoon freshly ground pepper
¼ cup shredded Gruyère or Swiss cheese
16 Niçoise or other oil-cured black olives

1. Trim any top ribs and the root end from the fennel bulb. Cut in half and cut out the hard center core. Either cut the fennel into very thin slices on a mandoline or coarsely shred in a food processor.

2. In a medium bowl, combine the fennel, orange slices, orange juice, lemon juice, extra virgin olive oil, salt and pepper. Toss until well mixed.

3. Arrange the fennel and orange slices on a serving plate. Pour all the juices from the bowl over them. Sprinkle the Gruyère cheese on top and garnish with the olives before serving.

Green Bean and Hazelnut Salad with Lemon Dijon Yogurt Dressing

This unusual and beautiful salad could easily make a light meal. In France, we would use tiny, sweet *haricots verts,* only about ¼ inch in diameter and about 2 inches long, which are very tender. Therefore, try to select the thinnest, smallest, sweetest green beans in your market for the best flavor.

4 SERVINGS   50% CALORIES FROM FAT   165 CALORIES PER SERVING

> ⅓ cup hazelnuts (filberts)
> 1 pound small green beans
> 8 small radicchio or butter lettuce leaves
> Lemon Dijon Yogurt Dressing (recipe follows)

1. Preheat the oven to 475° F. Spread out the hazelnuts in a small baking dish and toast in the oven 5 to 7 minutes, until the dark outer skins crack and the nuts are lightly browned. Remove to a plate and let cool. Coarsely chop the hazelnuts; there should be ¼ cup.

2. Trim the ends off the green beans, but leave them whole unless they are too large. In a large saucepan of boiling water, cook the green beans until just tender enough to bend slightly, 3 to 5 minutes. Drain and rinse under cold running water; drain well.

3. Arrange 2 radicchio leaves on each of 4 plates or use them to cover a platter. Mound the beans in the center. Drizzle the dressing over the beans and sprinkle the chopped hazelnuts over the top.

Lemon Dijon Yogurt Dressing

This is a lightened version of a traditional French cream-based dressing. You'll want to use this dressing over and over again, on tossed salads and steamed vegetables.

MAKES ABOUT 1¼ CUPS   49% CALORIES FROM FAT   54 CALORIES PER ¼ CUP

1 cup nonfat plain yogurt
2 tablespoons lemon juice
1 tablespoon Dijon mustard
1 teaspoon Asian sesame oil
2 teaspoons olive oil
⅛ teaspoon salt
Several grindings of black pepper

In a blender or a food processor, combine all of the above ingredients. Process until smooth. If not using at once, cover and refrigerate for up to 3 days.

Corsican Tomato, Cucumber, Mint and Feta Salad

Simplicity reigns in this French Corsican salad—sweet ripe tomatoes, crisp cucumbers and the mild saltiness of feta.

4 SERVINGS   56% CALORIES FROM FAT   127 CALORIES PER SERVING

2 large tomatoes, cut into ½-inch dice
2 large cucumbers, peeled, seeded and thinly sliced
3 ounces French or Greek feta cheese (about ¾ cup crumbled)
1 teaspoon lemon juice
1 tablespoon extra virgin olive oil
1 tablespoon finely shredded fresh mint
Freshly ground pepper

1. In a medium bowl, gently toss together the tomatoes and cucumbers to mix. Arrange the vegetables on a large serving plate.

2. Crumble the feta cheese over the tomatoes and cucumbers. Sprinkle the lemon juice and olive oil over the salad and garnish with the mint and a generous grinding of pepper.

Warm Chicken Breast Salad with Sherry Shallot Dressing

A typical chicken salad "French style" does not normally include the gobs of mayonnaise we are accustomed to. In fact, this warm salad, perfect for lunch or a light supper, contains just one tablespoon of oil and a scant ounce of bacon to boost the flavor.

4 SERVINGS   30% CALORIES FROM FAT   317 CALORIES PER SERVING

> *1 slice of lean bacon, cut into ¼-inch dice*
> *1⅓ pounds skinless, boneless chicken breast, cut crosswise into ½-inch slices*
> *2 tablespoons sherry wine vinegar*
> *⅛ teaspoon salt*
> *⅛ teaspoon freshly ground pepper*
> *1 pound mixed salad greens, rinsed, dried and torn into bite-size pieces*
> *Sherry Shallot Dressing (recipe follows) or 6 tablespoons of your favorite vinaigrette*
> *1⅓ cups Herbed Croutons, preferably homemade (page 48)*

1. Preheat the oven to 450° F. Bring a small saucepan of water to a boil over high heat. Add the bacon and cook 30 seconds. Drain and rinse briefly under running water. Pat dry on a paper towel.

2. Line an 8- or 9-inch square baking dish with aluminum foil, leaving plenty of overlap. Place the chicken and bacon in the dish and sprinkle on the vinegar, salt and pepper. Bring the edges of the foil together and crimp to seal tightly. Bake 10 to 15 minutes, or until the chicken is just white throughout but still juicy.

3. Meanwhile, place the greens in a medium bowl. Pour on the dressing and toss to coat. Divide the greens among 4 large plates.

4. Arrange the warm chicken slices over the salad greens and pour the bacon and any cooking juices from the pan over the chicken. Sprinkle ⅓ cup of croutons over each salad and serve.

Sherry Shallot Dressing

Sherry wine vinegar has a full-bodied, slightly sweet taste. This dressing is a good all-purpose vinaigrette for tossed salads and steamed vegetables and it also makes a fine marinade for grilled chicken and meats.

MAKES 6 TABLESPOONS   87% CALORIES FROM FAT   25 CALORIES PER TABLESPOON

> *1 tablespoon sherry wine vinegar*
> *1 tablespoon Dijon mustard*
> *1 tablespoon finely chopped shallots*
> *2 tablespoons reduced-sodium chicken broth*
> *2 teaspoons olive oil*
> *1 teaspoon Asian sesame oil*
> *Freshly ground pepper*

In a small bowl, whisk together the vinegar, mustard and shallots. Gradually whisk in the chicken broth, olive oil and sesame oil. Season with pepper to taste.

Mesclun Salad with Roasted Chèvre

Mesclun is a Provençal mixture of wild salad greens. It should include some bitter and sweet lettuces as well as tender and crisp greens. Assorted garden lettuces are becoming available in more and more supermarkets in the United States. A combination of Boston lettuce, chicory, radicchio and leaf lettuce can be substituted. Serve this salad as a light lunch or a first course at dinner.

4 SERVINGS   56% CALORIES FROM FAT   191 CALORIES PER SERVING

> *4 slices of French or Italian bread, cut ½ inch thick*
> *1 garlic clove, cut in half*
> *3 ounces creamy, mild goat cheese, such as Montrachet, cut into 4*
>   *rounds*
> *1 tablespoon extra virgin olive oil*
> *4 sprigs of fresh thyme or ¼ teaspoon dried thyme leaves*
> *Freshly ground black pepper*
> *1 pound mesclun or other mixed lettuces*
> *Dijon Vinaigrette (page 36) or ½ cup of your favorite vinaigrette*

1. Preheat the broiler. Lightly toast the bread either in a toaster or under the broiler. Rub the top side of the bread slices with the cut garlic clove.

2. Cut the toasted garlic bread in half diagonally and place a round of goat cheese on the widest part of each piece. Drizzle the olive oil over each piece of cheese. Top with a sprig of thyme and a generous grinding of pepper.

3. Set the toasts on a small baking sheet and broil about 6 inches from the heat 3 to 5 minutes, until the cheese is soft and begins to bubble.

4. In a medium mixing bowl, toss the mesclun with half of the vinaigrette until coated. Divide among 4 plates. Arrange a warm goat cheese toast on top of each salad and serve at once. Pass the remaining dressing on the side.

— *Potato and Frisée Salad with Hot Bacon and* — *Calvados Dressing*

French bacon and potato salad is a country classic—hearty, warming and full of earthy taste. Here is a version lightened with *frisée,* a bitter lettuce, and made affordable calorically and in terms of fat by using just a strip of bacon for flavor. Calvados is a French apple brandy; applejack or brandy can be substituted. Serve as a side salad or first course.

6 SERVINGS   38% CALORIES FROM FAT   164 CALORIES PER SERVING

> *1¼ pounds small red potatoes, scrubbed*
> *1 slice of lean bacon, cut into ¼-inch dice*
> *2 tablespoons sherry wine vinegar or red wine vinegar*
> *2 tablespoons Dijon mustard*
> *2 tablespoons minced shallots*
> *½ cup reduced-sodium chicken broth*
> *2 tablespoons olive oil*
> *¼ teaspoon salt*
> *⅛ teaspoon freshly ground pepper*
> *¾ pound frisée or chicory, rinsed, dried and torn into bite-size pieces*
> *1 tablespoon Calvados or applejack*

1. In a medium saucepan of boiling water, cook the potatoes until just tender, about 10 minutes. Drain and let cool, then cut into ¼-inch slices.

2. Meanwhile, bring a small saucepan of water to a boil. Add the bacon and cook 30 seconds. Drain and rinse briefly under running water. Pat dry on a paper towel.

3. In a blender or food processor, combine the vinegar, mustard, shallots, chicken broth and olive oil. Process until the dressing is smooth and well blended.

4. In a large nonstick skillet, combine half of the dressing with the potatoes and bacon. Cook over high heat, stirring gently and turning with a spatula, until the potatoes begin to get crusty on the bottom, about 5 minutes. Season with the salt and pepper. Remove from the heat and cover to keep warm.

5. Put the frisée in a medium heatproof bowl. In a small nonreactive saucepan, combine the remaining dressing with the Calvados. Bring to a boil and pour over the greens. Toss to coat.

6. Divide the frisée among 4 plates. Top with the hot potato salad and serve at once.

Hearts of Romaine with Lemon Honey-Date Dressing

The Moroccan influence is strong in this refreshing salad. It can easily be turned into a main course by adding some thinly sliced chicken breast and Lemon Confit (page 144). Goat or feta cheeses are also appealing on this salad.

4 SERVINGS   28% CALORIES FROM FAT   114 CALORIES PER SERVING

3 tablespoons lemon juice
1 tablespoon honey
1 tablespoon extra virgin olive oil
¼ teaspoon cinnamon
¼ cup chopped (¼-inch) pitted dates
1 teaspoon chopped cilantro or parsley
Salt and freshly ground pepper
1 small head of romaine lettuce, torn into bite-size pieces
1 navel orange, peeled and thinly sliced

1. In a small bowl, combine the lemon juice, honey, olive oil and cinnamon. Whisk until blended. Stir in the dates and cilantro. Season the dressing with salt and pepper to taste.

2. In a medium mixing bowl, combine the romaine with the dressing and toss until coated. Divide the salad among 4 plates, garnish with the orange slices and serve.

Smoked Fish Salad with Capers, Pickled Red Onions and Spinach

This salad is a personal favorite. I particularly enjoy the rich smoky flavor and the buttery texture of the fish in contrast to the crispness of the greens and the sweetness of the onions. Serve as a light lunch or as an elegant starter to a special meal.

4 SERVINGS   36% CALORIES FROM FAT   129 CALORIES PER SERVING

½ pound washed leaf spinach, ready to use
Sherry Shallot Dressing (page 69) or 6 tablespoons of your favorite
  vinaigrette
3 ounces smoked salmon, shredded
3 ounces smoked whitefish, coarsely flaked
3 ounces smoked sable, coarsely flaked
1 large sweet onion, preferably red, finely slivered
1 tablespoon capers, rinsed and drained

1. In a medium bowl, toss the spinach with half of the vinaigrette and divide among 4 serving plates.

2. Arrange the smoked salmon, whitefish and sable on top of the spinach, dividing evenly.

3. Sprinkle 2 tablespoons slivered onion and ¾ teaspoon capers over each salad and drizzle the remaining vinaigrette on top.

Warm Roasted Salmon Salad with Mesclun, Potato, Onion and Bacon

Roasting salmon brings out its rich flavor, which is enhanced here with sherry vinegar and a touch of smoky bacon. This main-course salad can be served warm or at room temperature.

4 SERVINGS   52% CALORIES FROM FAT   293 CALORIES PER SERVING

½ pound small red potatoes, scrubbed
1 slice of lean bacon, cut into ¼-inch dice
12 ounces skinless salmon fillet, cut into 4 equal pieces
1 teaspoon extra virgin olive oil
2 tablespoons sherry wine vinegar
2 tablespoons reduced-sodium chicken broth
Salt and freshly ground pepper
½ pound mesclun or other mixed lettuces
1 small red onion, thinly sliced
1 double recipe Sherry Shallot Dressing (page 69) or ¾ cup of your
    favorite vinaigrette

1. Preheat the oven to 450° F. Place the potatoes in a medium saucepan, add water to cover by at least 1 inch and bring to a boil. Reduce the heat to medium and cook 10 to 15 minutes, until the potatoes are tender throughout. Drain, rinse under cold water and set aside to cool.

2. Meanwhile, bring a small saucepan of water to a boil. Add the bacon and cook 30 seconds. Drain and rinse briefly under running water. Pat dry on a paper towel.

3. Place the fish in a nonstick 8- or 9-inch baking dish. Rub the pieces of salmon with the extra virgin olive oil. Sprinkle the bacon, vinegar and chicken broth over the fish and season lightly with salt and pepper to taste. Roast the salmon about 10 minutes, or until just opaque throughout.

4. Meanwhile, slice the cooked potatoes (I like to leave the skins on for color). In a medium bowl, combine the potatoes, mesclun, and red onion. Pour on half the vinaigrette and toss to mix. Divide the salad among 4 large plates.

5. Top each salad with a piece of roasted salmon and drizzle the remaining vinaigrette over the fish. Serve at once.

Salade Niçoise

Salade Niçoise, naturally light and very satisfying, is definitely a meal in itself. Some crusty bread, about 100 calories per slice, is a must as an accompaniment.

4 SERVINGS   33% CALORIES FROM FAT   397 CALORIES PER SERVING

> *1 pound small red potatoes, scrubbed*
> *½ pound green beans, trimmed and halved if large*
> *Dijon Vinaigrette (page 36)*
> *1 teaspoon finely chopped garlic*
> *1 cup canned low-salt chick peas, rinsed and drained*
> *1 small head of romaine lettuce, torn into pieces*
> *1 can (6⅛ ounces) water-packed tuna, drained and flaked*
> *12 Niçoise or other oil-cured black olives*
> *2 hard-boiled eggs, halved*
> *4 plum tomatoes, quartered*
> *8 anchovy fillets, rinsed and drained*

1. In a medium saucepan of boiling water, cook the potatoes over high heat until fork tender, 8 to 10 minutes. Drain and let cool. Then cut into quarters.

2. Meanwhile, in another saucepan of boiling water, cook the green beans until tender enough to bend slightly, 5 to 7 minutes. Drain and rinse under cold running water; drain well.

3. In a large bowl, stir together the vinaigrette and garlic. Add the potatoes, green beans, chick peas and romaine lettuce. Toss until the vegetables are well coated with the dressing.

4. Mound the salad onto a large platter. Arrange the tuna, olives, eggs, tomatoes and anchovy fillets on top and serve.

Poached Scallop Salad with Champagne Cumin Vinaigrette and Roasted Red Peppers

This colorful salad is a beautiful and light way to start off a special meal; or, serve on its own, as an entree.

4 SERVINGS   27% CALORIES FROM FAT   163 CALORIES PER SERVING

1 pound whole bay scallops or halved sea scallops
Champagne Cumin Vinaigrette (recipe follows)
½ pound mixed lettuces, such as Boston, red leaf and frisée
½ recipe Roasted Red Peppers (page 34) or 1 jar (8 ounces) roasted
red pepper strips, drained

1. Place the scallops in a steamer basket or stainless steel strainer. Set in a saucepan over simmering water, cover and steam 1 to 2 minutes, or until just opaque throughout.

2. Drain the scallops and place them in a medium bowl. Pour 3 tablespoons of the vinaigrette over the hot scallops and toss to mix. Let cool slightly, then cover and refrigerate until chilled, at least 2 hours.

3. In a medium bowl, combine the greens with 3 more tablespoons vinaigrette and toss to mix well. Divide the lettuces among 4 large plates. Mound the scallops on top and garnish with the strips of roasted pepper. Pass the remaining dressing on the side.

Champagne Cumin Vinaigrette

The delicate fruitiness of champagne vinegar and earthiness of cumin with a heavy dose of Dijon mustard form an inspired partnership that is delicious on almost any kind of fish or seafood. This dressing also goes well with chicken, green beans, carrots and chick peas.

MAKES ABOUT ¾ CUP   85% CALORIES FROM FAT   26 CALORIES PER TABLESPOON

¼ cup champagne vinegar or other white wine vinegar
¼ cup reduced-sodium chicken broth
2 tablespoons olive oil
2 tablespoons Dijon mustard
2 tablespoons finely chopped shallots
1 teaspoon ground cumin
Salt and freshly ground pepper

In a blender or a food processor, combine the vinegar, chicken broth, olive oil, mustard, shallots and cumin. Process until smooth and well blended. Season with salt and pepper to taste.

— *Grilled Shrimp with Roasted Orange Thyme* — *Vinaigrette and Mesclun*

The art of salad making in France is endless. This flavorful combination hails from the sunny south of France, where it would make the evening meal.

4 SERVINGS   21% CALORIES FROM FAT   237 CALORIES PER SERVING

1 pound medium shrimp, shelled and deveined
Salt and freshly ground pepper
½ cup orange juice
1 pound mesclun (mixed baby greens) or mixed salad greens
Roasted Orange Thyme Vinaigrette (recipe follows)

1. Light a hot fire in a charcoal grill or preheat the broiler. Season the shrimp lightly with salt and pepper. Set them on a grill rack or broiler pan and grill or broil about 4 inches from the heat, turning once and basting frequently with the orange juice, 3 to 4 minutes, or until the shrimp are lightly browned, curled and opaque throughout.

2. Meanwhile, in a medium mixing bowl, toss the greens with half of the vinaigrette. Divide the salad among 4 plates.

3. Remove the shrimp from the grill and toss with the remaining vinaigrette. Arrange on top of the greens and serve at once.

Roasted Orange Thyme Vinaigrette

With its whole slices of orange and sweet onion, this is a dressing with substance, even though it is so light in fat. Try it with scallops, poached fish and grilled chicken as well.

4 SERVINGS   30% CALORIES FROM FAT   105 CALORIES PER SERVING

2 seedless oranges, sliced paper thin
1 medium red onion, thinly sliced
1 large shallot, thinly sliced
2 garlic cloves, thinly sliced
8 sprigs of fresh thyme or ½ teaspoon dried thyme leaves
1 tablespoon extra virgin olive oil
¾ cup freshly squeezed orange juice
2 tablespoons lemon juice
2 tablespoons reduced-sodium chicken broth
1 tablespoon chopped parsley
1 teaspoon sugar
Salt and freshly ground pepper

1. Preheat the oven to 400° F. Place the orange slices, red onion, shallot, garlic and thyme in the center of a sheet of aluminum foil and toss to mix. Drizzle the olive oil over all. Bring up the edges of the foil and twist the edges together into a packet. Place in a small baking dish and roast in the oven 30 minutes, or until the onion is tender. If using fresh thyme, remove and discard the sprigs.

2. In a small bowl, combine the orange juice, lemon juice, chicken broth, parsley and sugar. Whisk until blended. Stir in the roasted orange base and season with salt and pepper to taste.

FISH
AND
SHELLFISH

Historically, seafood was the primary "meat" of the French poor, because it was so abundant and easily available to anyone industrious—or hungry—enough to go fishing. Meat was always more dear and, consequently, less featured in peasant cooking. In French country cooking, the fish and seafood of each region is prepared in unique ways. Just as fish and seafood are flavored by the water in which they live, these dishes reflect the flavors and ingredients of the particular region in which they originated.

The seafood cooking techniques featured here are low in fat, quick and succinct. While roasting, grilling, poaching and baking are techniques naturally low in calories, it is what's served with the fish that tips the scale. In French country cooking, "saucing the fish" means enhancing the natural delicate flavor and texture of the fish, not masking them with heavy, flour-thickened butter and cream sauces. Homestyle cooking favors vinaigrette-based sauces, fragrant purees of basil, watercress, arugula or mint, or light "*coulis,*" or purees of tomato or red pepper. Citrus-based orange or lemon juice sauces as well as the traditionally fiery condiments, such as rouille or harissa sauce, are also very common.

Poaching fish (as in Poached Salmon Trout with Aromatic Vegetables or Red Snapper Goujonettes à la Barigoule) is the lightest and most delicately flavored of all preparations. Here the fish is poached in a light aromatic *fumet,* or broth, until it is just firm to the touch. Delicious warm or cold, fish cooked in this way is characteristically light, moist and succulent.

Grilling or broiling fish—as in Grilled Tuna with Anchovy Sauce, Shrimp and Scallop Brochettes with Fresh Basil and Broiled Sole à l'Orange—quickly seals in the juices. Only a light brushing of olive oil to prevent sticking is needed. In grilling fish, always make sure that your grill rack is ultra clean and that the fish is not cold from the refrigerator before grilling; this will also help prevent sticking.

In dishes like Scallops Baked with Garlic, Tomatoes, Wine and Bread Crumbs and Baked Red Snapper Catalane, the fish or seafood is cooked with vegetables, which require very little fat and contribute a whole lot of flavor. Roasted fish, such as Roasted Halibut Steaks with Herbed Citrus Vinaigrette and Roasted Salmon with Sherry Wine Vinegar and Marinated Lentils, work best if quickly roasted in a hot (450° F.) oven. The high heat quickly cooks the fish as it seals the juices inside.

Seafood stews, such as the ethereal Shrimp "à la Nage" with Spinach and Vegetable Julienne, homey Bouillabaisse of Clams, Spinach, Potato and Saffron Broth and the spectacular French classics, such as Mussels Marinière Steamed with Wine and Aromatic Vegetables, Bouillabaisse and Choucroute Garnie Marinière, are festive dishes, that are downright opulent considering how calorically affordable they have been made.

There is even a recipe for a delicious Shrimp and Scallop Mousse with Watercress Cream, which is excellent warm or cold. The smooth, delectable mousse contains no egg yolks, butter, cream or flour—just the delicate flavor of the sea.

Halibut en Papillote with Lemon

Cooking in paper literally steams the fish with little or no fat necessary. Place all of the ingredients and seasonings in the packet and they will create their own juice. Fish and chicken come out moist and flavorful. Best of all, there are no messy pans to clean up.

4 SERVINGS   26% CALORIES FROM FAT   219 CALORIES PER SERVING

2 teaspoons extra virgin olive oil
2 lemons, thinly sliced
4 garlic cloves, thinly sliced
½ teaspoon fennel seeds
4 sprigs of fresh thyme or ¼ teaspoon dried thyme leaves
4 sprigs of parsley
4 halibut steaks, cut ½ inch thick (6 ounces each)
Salt and freshly ground pepper
½ cup white vermouth or dry white wine

1. Preheat the oven to 400° F. Cut 4 heart shapes about 10 inches tall and 8 inches wide out of aluminum foil, parchment or wax paper. Brush each heart with ½ teaspoon of the olive oil.

2. Divide the lemon, garlic, fennel, thyme and parsley among the papillotes, covering only one side of the hearts. Set a fish steak on each and season lightly with salt and pepper to taste. Pour 2 tablespoons vermouth over each piece of fish.

3. Fold over the edges of the foil or paper and crimp to seal tightly. Put the packets on a baking sheet. Bake 10 to 12 minutes, or until the fish is opaque throughout but still juicy. (You may have to open one carefully to test.)

4. To serve, transfer the fish from the packets to dinner plates. Pour the cooking juices from the packets over the fish.

Roasted Halibut Steaks with Herbed Citrus Vinaigrette

Sea bass, scrod, red snapper or any other firm white-fleshed fish can be substituted for the halibut. Serve this dish with Provençal Lemon Herb Rice (page 161) and steamed zucchini.

4 Servings   30% Calories from fat   217 Calories per serving

2 tablespoons chopped shallots
4 halibut steaks, cut 1/2 inch thick (6 ounces each)
1/4 cup white vermouth or dry white wine
1/4 cup reduced-sodium chicken broth
8 sprigs of fresh thyme or 1 teaspoon dried thyme leaves
1/4 teaspoon salt
1/8 teaspoon freshly ground pepper
Herbed Citrus Vinaigrette (recipe follows)

1. Preheat the oven to 450° F. Sprinkle the shallots over the bottom of a shallow baking dish just large enough to fit all of the halibut steaks in a single layer. Place the fish on top. Pour the vermouth and chicken broth over the fish. Season with the thyme, salt and pepper.

2. Transfer to the oven and roast the fish, uncovered, 10 to 12 minutes, until just opaque in the center.

3. With a slotted spoon, transfer the fish to serving plates. Spoon one-fourth of the vinaigrette over each hot fish steak and serve at once.

Herbed Citrus Vinaigrette

This recipe for herbed citrus vinaigrette is another family favorite. It is excellent on any kind of poached, grilled, baked or broiled fish served warm or at room temperature.

MAKES ABOUT ⅔ CUP   62% CALORIES FROM FAT   21 CALORIES PER TABLESPOON

1 tablespoon Dijon mustard
½ cup orange juice
1 teaspoon grated lemon zest
1 tablespoon lemon juice
1 tablespoon extra virgin olive oil
2 scallions, thinly sliced
1 tablespoon chopped parsley
⅛ teaspoon salt
⅛ teaspoon freshly ground pepper

In a medium bowl, whisk together the mustard, orange juice, lemon zest, lemon juice and olive oil until blended. Stir in the scallions and parsley. Season with the salt and pepper.

— *Mussels Marinière Steamed with Wine and* — *Aromatic Vegetables*

Mussels Marinière is always a favorite on both sides of the Atlantic. This variation is hearty with chunks of aromatic vegetables and fragrant seasonings. Serve with slices of Toasted Garlic Bread (page 51).

Leftover broth can be turned into a delicious fish soup by adding any kind of fish and some boiled potatoes; try it chunky or puree it.

6 SERVINGS   28% CALORIES FROM FAT   249 CALORIES PER SERVING

1 tablespoon olive oil
1 cup diced (¼-inch) onions
1 cup diced (¼-inch) carrots
1 cup diced (¼-inch) zucchini
1 cup diced (¼-inch) fennel
1 cup diced (¼-inch) green bell peppers
2 cups dry white wine or white vermouth
1 tablespoon capers, drained
6 sprigs of fresh thyme or ½ teaspoon dried thyme leaves
2 tablespoons finely chopped garlic
6 pounds mussels, scrubbed and debearded
1 tablespoon chopped parsley
1 tablespoon shredded fresh basil (optional)
1 teaspoon minced lemon zest

1. In a large pot, heat the olive oil. Add the onions, carrots, zucchini, fennel and green peppers, cover and cook over medium heat, stirring occasionally, until the vegetables are tender, about 15 minutes.

2. Pour in the wine and add the capers, thyme, half of the garlic and the mussels. Toss well. Cover and cook over high heat until the mussels open, 5 to 7 minutes. Discard any mussels that do not open.

3. In a small bowl, combine the remaining garlic with the parsley, basil and lemon zest.

4. Divide the mussels, vegetables and broth among 4 individual serving bowls. Sprinkle some of the garlic/herb mixture over each portion.

Roasted Salmon with
Sherry Wine Vinegar and Marinated Lentils

In this country, we are not as used to serving beans with fish as the French are, but the rich meat of the salmon is complemented beautifully by the earthiness of the lentils. When I use this dish for entertaining, I like to accompany it with half a recipe of Chiffonade of Red Cabbage (page 24), both because of the color combination and because the lentils and the cabbage can be prepared well ahead of time. This is a simple method for pan-roasting salmon; the fish itself can also be served with steamed asparagus or another green vegetable.

4 Servings   41% Calories from fat   373 Calories per serving

> 4 salmon steaks, cut ½ inch thick, skinned and boned (6 ounces each)
> Salt and freshly ground pepper
> 1 tablespoon olive oil
> ¼ cup sherry wine vinegar
> ½ recipe Marinated Lentils (page 32), prepared through step 2, at
>   room temperature
> 4 sprigs of parsley
> 4 lemon wedges

1. Preheat the oven to 400° F. Season the salmon fillets lightly with salt and pepper.

2. Heat the olive oil in a large nonstick skillet with an ovenproof handle or in a 10-inch flameproof gratin. Add the salmon steaks and cook over medium-high heat, until browned on the bottom, about 2 minutes. Flip the steaks over, add the vinegar to the pan and transfer to the oven.

3. Roast the salmon 10 minutes, or until the fish is just cooked through and opaque to the center.

4. To serve, place one-fourth of the lentils in the center of each plate. Set a salmon steak on top of the lentils and garnish the rim of each plate with a sprig of parsley and a lemon wedge.

Broiled Salmon Paillard with Meaux Mustard Sauce

Moutarde de Meaux is a mild, grainy mustard that has a wonderful mellow flavor. It is a pleasant change from the hot Dijon style. Any whole-grain mustard can be substituted. Meaux mustard cream is another useful sauce. Spread it on fish or chicken before broiling or baking, or heat gently and toss with pasta or vegetables. I've even used it instead of mayonnaise mixed into chicken salad or as a sandwich spread. Note: If you are leery of slicing the salmon thin enough, ask your fishmonger to do it for you.

4 SERVINGS   42% CALORIES FROM FAT   306 CALORIES PER SERVING

3 tablespoons Meaux mustard or other mild whole-grain mustard
1 cup nonfat plain yogurt
1 tablespoon lemon juice
½ teaspoon salt
¼ teaspoon freshly ground pepper
2 teaspoons extra virgin olive oil
1½ pounds salmon fillet, skinned and thinly sliced crosswise on the diagonal into slices no more than ½ inch thick

1. In a small mixing bowl, combine the mustard, yogurt, lemon juice and half the salt and pepper. Blend together until smooth.

2. Preheat the broiler. Brush a nonstick baking dish with the extra virgin olive oil and arrange the salmon slices in a single layer on the dish. Season with the remaining salt and pepper. Spoon 2 tablespoons of the mustard sauce onto the center of each salmon paillard.

3. Broil about 4 inches from the heat, without turning, 5 minutes, or until the sauce bubbles and the fish is just opaque throughout. Serve at once. Pass the remaining mustard sauce on the side.

Grilled Tuna with Anchovy Sauce

Anchovies are a favorite condiment in Provence. This sauce appears rustic, but it is subtle when lightly brushed on fish, meats and vegetables.

4 SERVINGS   43% CALORIES FROM FAT   286 CALORIES PER SERVING

> 1 can (2 ounces) anchovies, drained and rinsed
> 1 garlic clove, crushed through a press
> 6 Mediterranean-style or other oil-cured black olives, pitted and finely
>   chopped
> 1 tablespoon chopped parsley
> 2 tablespoons lemon juice
> ¼ cup reduced-sodium chicken broth
> 1 tablespoon capers, rinsed and drained
> ⅛ teaspoon freshly ground pepper
> 4 tuna steaks, cut ½ inch thick (6 ounces each)
> 1 tablespoon extra virgin olive oil

1. Light a hot fire in a charcoal grill or preheat the broiler. In a food processor or blender, combine the anchovies, garlic, olives, parsley, lemon juice, chicken broth, capers and pepper. Puree until smooth. Set the anchovy sauce aside.

2. Brush the tuna steaks with the extra virgin olive oil and grill or broil about 4 inches from the heat, turning once, 10 to 12 minutes, until just opaque throughout but still juicy.

3. To serve, spoon 1 tablespoon of anchovy sauce over each tuna steak and brush to coat evenly. Pass the remaining sauce on the side.

Shrimp "à la Nage" with Spinach and Vegetable Julienne

A la nage ("swimming") is a poetic term for seafood dishes that contain a large proportion of broth—somewhere between a soup and a light stew. This unusual dish's strong visual appeal, contrast of textures, delicate flavors and lightness will surely please the strictest of weight watchers. The trick here is to cut the vegetables as thinly as possible so they will cook at the same time as the shrimp do. For the thinnest cuts, use a mandoline or the fine julienne blade on a food processor; or cut by hand. The spinach is cut into thin strips and cooks instantaneously when the broth is poured over it. This is what the French would call *cuisine santé:* healthy cooking.

4 SERVINGS   27% CALORIES FROM FAT   236 CALORIES PER SERVING

> *1 tablespoon extra virgin olive oil*
> *1½ pounds large shrimp, shelled and deveined, shells reserved*
> *¼ cup minced shallots*
> *2 tablespoons brandy*
> *2 cans (14½ ounces each) reduced-sodium chicken broth*
> *½ teaspoon ground coriander*
> *2 tablespoons peeled and minced fresh ginger*
> *8 whole black peppercorns*
> *1 medium leek (white part only), cut into ¼-inch-thick strips*
> *1 medium carrot, cut into ¼-inch-thick strips*
> *½ small zucchini (about 2 ounces), cut into ¼-inch-thick strips*
> *½ pound fresh spinach leaves, cut into ¼-inch-wide strips*
> *1 tablespoon chopped chives*

1. In a medium saucepan, heat the olive oil. Add the shrimp shells and shallots and cook over medium-high heat, stirring often, until the shells turn bright red and the shallots are soft and golden, 3 to 5 minutes.

2. Add the brandy and carefully ignite with a match. When the flames subside, pour in the chicken broth and 4 cups of water. Add the coriander, ginger and peppercorns. Bring to a boil, lower the heat and simmer the shrimp stock 30 to 45 minutes.

3. Pour the shrimp stock through a fine-mesh strainer into a heatproof bowl and set aside. (The recipe can be made to this point up to 2 days in advance. Cover and refrigerate the stock.)

4. Reheat the shrimp stock in a medium saucepan. When it reaches a simmer, add the shrimp, leek, carrot and zucchini. Cook over medium heat just until the shrimp turn pink and curl, 2 to 3 minutes.

5. Mound 1 cup of the sliced spinach in each of 4 soup plates. Arrange the shrimp over the spinach, spoon some of the vegetable julienne in the center of each bowl and finish by pouring the stock over all. Garnish with the chives and serve at once.

Shrimp and Scallop Brochettes with Fresh Basil

Outdoor grilling is popular in the French countryside. Here skewered shrimp and scallops are barbecued with a garlicky basil sauce. Serve these brochettes on a bed of Provençal Lemon Herb Rice (page 161).

4 Servings   21% Calories from fat   212 Calories per serving

½ cup packed fresh basil leaves
1 garlic clove, crushed through a press
¼ cup reduced-sodium chicken broth
2 tablespoons white vermouth or dry white wine
2 teaspoons extra virgin olive oil
⅛ teaspoon salt
⅛ teaspoon freshly ground pepper
16 medium shrimp (about ¾ pound), shelled and deveined
16 large sea scallops, trimmed

1. Light a hot fire in a charcoal grill or preheat the broiler. In a blender or food processor, combine the basil, garlic, chicken broth, vermouth, olive oil, salt and pepper. Puree until smooth.

2. Pour half the basil sauce into a medium bowl. Add the shrimp and scallops and toss to coat. Alternate shrimp and scallops on brochette skewers. (If using wooden ones, make sure to soak them in water for at least 10 minutes before using to prevent charring.)

3. Grill or broil the brochettes, turning, 5 to 8 minutes, until the seafood is lightly browned outside and just opaque throughout. Brush the remaining basil sauce over the brochettes and serve at once.

Shrimp and Scallop Mousse with Watercress Cream

Traditionally, seafood mousses are bound with cream and egg yolks, while others might include butter and flour as well. This version doesn't contain a bit of these fatty, high-calorie ingredients. A truly delicious, exceptionally light mousse is created by relying on the natural gelatinous properties of fish and shellfish, with the addition of nonfat dry milk and egg whites. Depending on how you wish to serve this dish, it can be presented hot or cold.

6 TO 8 SERVINGS   16% CALORIES FROM FAT   187 CALORIES PER SERVING

3 egg whites
½ pound shrimp, shelled and deveined
½ pound scallops
½ pound flounder fillets
½ cup nonfat dry milk
½ teaspoon ground coriander
½ teaspoon salt
¼ teaspoon white pepper
1¼ cups ice water
2 teaspoons olive oil
Watercress Cream (recipe follows)
½ pound plum tomatoes (3 or 4), seeded and finely diced

1. Preheat the oven to 250° F. In a medium bowl, beat the egg whites until stiff and glossy.

2. In a food processor, combine the shrimp, scallops and flounder. Puree until smooth. Add the dry milk, coriander, salt and white pepper and blend well. With the machine on, pour in the ice water through the feed tube.

3. Place the beaten egg whites on top of the seafood puree and pulse until the egg whites are just blended in; do not overmix.

4. Grease a 9 × 5 × 3-inch loaf pan with the olive oil. Pack the seafood mixture into the loaf pan. (Make sure the mousse is packed down to press out any air holes.) Cover with a piece of greased parchment or wax paper.

5. Bake 1 hour 45 minutes, or until a knife inserted into the center of the loaf comes out clean. Transfer to a rack and let the mousse cool 30 minutes. Then unmold onto a platter and serve warm or cover and refrigerate until chilled.

6. To serve, cut into ½-inch slices and spoon about ¼ cup of the watercress cream next to or over the mousse. Garnish each plate with one-fourth of the diced tomatoes. Pass the remaining watercress cream on the side.

Watercress Cream

There's no cream in this sauce. It achieves its body from a light puree of potatoes. Watercress cream is very tasty hot or cold, on all kinds of fish or chicken. Use it in place of green mayonnaise.

Makes 2½ to 3 cups   7% Calories from fat   31 Calories per ¹ ₄ cup

2 large bunches of watercress, washed
1 large baking potato (½ pound), peeled and cut into 1-inch chunks
6 garlic cloves
2 tablespoons finely chopped shallots
1 can (14½ ounches (reduced-sodium chicken broth
1 teaspoon finely chopped lemon zest
2 tablespoons lemon juice
½ to 1 cup nonfat milk
Salt and freshly ground pepper

1. Remove all of the large stems from the watercress and rinse well. Plunge the watercress into a large saucepan of boiling water and cook 30 seconds. Drain well and set aside.

2. In a medium saucepan, combine the potato, garlic, shallots and chicken broth. Bring to a boil and cook over medium heat until the potato is soft, about 10 minutes. Drain into a colander.

3. In a food processor, combine the potato, watercress, lemon zest and lemon juice. Puree until smooth. Add enough milk to thin the cream to the consistency of sour cream. Season with salt and pepper to taste. Serve hot or chilled.

Scallops Baked with Garlic, Tomatoes, Wine and Bread Crumbs

In this Coquilles Saint-Jacques Provençal-style, tomatoes, garlic and olive oil replace the typical heavy, roux-based, cheese-laden Mornay sauce. The effect is so light and delicious you'll never miss the calories. Personally, I've always preferred this version, because the sweet flavor of the scallops isn't masked by a heavy sauce. For a complete main course, serve with Provençal Lemon Herb Rice (page 161) and steamed spinach.

4 SERVINGS   21% CALORIES FROM FAT   257 CALORIES PER SERVING

1½ pounds sea scallops, cleaned and trimmed
1 tablespoon finely chopped garlic
2 medium tomatoes, peeled, seeded and chopped, or 1 cup chopped,
   drained low-sodium canned tomatoes
¼ cup dry white wine or white vermouth
1 tablespoon chopped parsley
1 tablespoon shredded fresh basil
¼ teaspoon salt
⅛ teaspoon freshly ground pepper
½ cup plain bread crumbs
1 tablespoon extra virgin olive oil

1. Preheat the oven to 450° F. In a medium bowl, combine the scallops, garlic, tomatoes, wine, parsley, basil, salt and pepper. Stir until the scallops are well coated.

2. Pour the contents of the bowl into a 12-inch oval gratin or an 8 × 11-inch baking dish. Sprinkle the bread crumbs on top and drizzle the olive oil over the crumbs.

3. Bake 10 to 15 minutes, or until the scallops are just opaque throughout and the crumbs are nicely browned.

Baked Sole Roulades with Zucchini and Red Pepper Coulis

Festive fish roulades are perfect for entertaining, because they can be prepared ahead of time and baked at the last moment. These are particularly attractive with the pale green zucchini and bright red pepper puree. Serve with steamed rice and a salad.

4 SERVINGS   24% CALORIES FROM FAT   227 CALORIES PER SERVING

> *1 pound zucchini, scrubbed*
> *1 tablespoon olive oil*
> *2 garlic cloves, finely chopped*
> *½ teaspoon fresh thyme leaves or ¼ teaspoon dried*
> *1 tablespoon finely shredded basil*
> *4 fillets of sole or flounder (6 ounces each)*
> *Salt and freshly ground pepper*
> *¼ cup reduced-sodium chicken broth*
> *1 tablespoon white vermouth or white wine*
> *½ teaspoon ground cumin*
> *Red Pepper Coulis (recipe follows)*

1. Preheat the oven to 400° F. Cut the zucchini into fine julienne strips or coarsely shred in a food processor.

2. Heat the olive oil in a large nonstick skillet. Add the zucchini and garlic and cook over medium-high heat, stirring occasionally, 3 to 5 minutes, or until just tender. Stir in the thyme and basil and remove from the heat.

3. Season the fish fillets lightly with salt and pepper. Divide the zucchini filling among the fillets, spreading to cover evenly. Roll up each fillet like a jelly roll.

4. Pour the chicken broth in a small baking dish, place the roulades, seam side-down, in the dish and pour the wine over the roulades. Bake 20 to 30 minutes, or until the fish is just cooked through and flakes easily.

5. Stir the cumin into the red pepper coulis. Transfer the fish to serving plates and spoon about 3 tablespoons over each portion.

NOTE *To prepare the roulades ahead of time, complete the recipe through step 3. Place the roulades on a plate, cover with plastic wrap and refrigerate until ready to use. Continue with the recipe starting with step 4.*

Red Pepper Coulis

You'll find that this bright red puree is a very useful sauce—whether you use it as a base for a dip, spread over grilled fish or meat, or stirred into a cream sauce or a soup. It adds body and lots of flavor with practically no calories.

MAKES ABOUT ¾ CUP   7% CALORIES FROM FAT   6 CALORIES PER TABLESPOON

> *½ recipe Roasted Red Peppers (page 34) or 8 ounces jarred roasted*
> *peppers, drained*
> *1 tablespoon lemon juice*
> *2 garlic cloves, crushed through a press*
> *Salt and freshly ground pepper*

In a blender or food processor, combine the roasted peppers, lemon juice and garlic. Puree until smooth. Season with salt and pepper to taste.

Choucroute Garnie Marinière

When fish and shellfish are used in a *choucroute garnie* in place of heavy, fat-laden pork products and smoked meats, the result is much healthier and infinitely lighter, yet still satisfying and full of flavor. While sauerkraut and seafood may sound like an odd combination, they go together beautifully, producing what is, in fact, a very tasty, quite elegant dish, most appropriate for entertaining.

6 TO 8 SERVINGS   30% CALORIES FROM FAT   204 CALORIES PER SERVING

1 slice of lean bacon, cut into ¼-inch dice
1 tablespoon olive oil
½ cup finely diced onion
½ cup finely diced carrots
2 pounds sauerkraut, preferably the refrigerated type, drained
1 bay leaf
4 sprigs of parsley plus 1 tablespoon chopped parsley
4 sprigs of fresh thyme or ¼ teaspoon dried thyme leaves
½ teaspoon caraway seeds
8 whole cloves
10 juniper berries
4 cups dry white wine
1 pound monkfish fillets, cut into 2-inch pieces
2 pounds mussels, scrubbed and debearded
½ pound shrimp, shelled and deveined
4 ounces smoked salmon, cut into ¼-inch strips

1. Bring a small saucepan of water to a boil over high heat. Add the bacon and cook 30 seconds. Drain, rinse briefly and drain well.

2. In a large flameproof casserole, heat the olive oil. Add the bacon, onion and carrots, cover and cook over medium-low heat, stirring occasionally, until the vegetables are tender, 8 to 10 minutes.

3. Add the sauerkraut, bay leaf, parsley sprigs, thyme, caraway, cloves, juniper berries and wine. Bring to a boil, reduce the heat to medium-low and simmer, stirring occasionally, until the sauerkraut is tender and most of the wine has been absorbed, about 40 minutes.

4. Add the monkfish, raise the heat to medium and cook 5 minutes. Add the mussels, cover the pan and cook until they just begin to open, 3 to 5 minutes. Add the shrimp and cook until pink and loosely curled, 2 to 3 minutes longer.

5. Mound the choucroute on a large platter and arrange the strips of smoked salmon attractively on top. Sprinkle with the chopped parsley and serve at once.

Baked Red Snapper Catalane

Spanish influence crops up in many country French dishes, and here it is evident in the savory vegetable mélange that serves as a bed for the snapper fillets. Peppers, tomatoes, zucchini and onion, cooked in just one tablespoon of good olive oil, make this a very light, nutritious preparation. Any firm, white fish, such as halibut, scrod, sea bass or monkfish fillets, can be substituted for the red snapper.

4 SERVINGS   24% CALORIES FROM FAT   270 CALORIES PER SERVING

1 tablespoon plus 1 teaspoon extra virgin olive oil
2 medium green bell peppers, thinly sliced
1 medium onion, thinly sliced
2 medium zucchini, thinly sliced
3 garlic cloves, finely chopped
4 sprigs of fresh thyme or ¼ teaspoon dried thyme leaves
1 can (14 ounces) low-salt chopped tomatoes, drained
½ teaspoon cayenne pepper
½ teaspoon salt
¼ teaspoon freshly ground pepper
4 red snapper fillets, ½ inch thick (6 ounces each)
1 lemon, thinly sliced
1 tablespoon chopped parsley
1 tablespoon finely shredded basil

1. In a large nonstick skillet, heat 1 tablespoon of the extra virgin olive oil. Add the peppers, onion, zucchini and garlic, cover and cook over medium heat 3 minutes. Uncover and cook, stirring occasionally, until the vegetables are just tender, 5 to 7 minutes longer.

2. Add the thyme, tomatoes, cayenne, and half the salt and pepper. Reduce the heat to medium-low and simmer, uncovered, 15 minutes, until most of the tomato juices have evaporated. Meanwhile, preheat the oven to 400° F.

3. Pour the vegetable mélange into a shallow 8 × 11-inch baking dish or 12-inch oval gratin. Arrange the red snapper fillets on top in a single layer. Season with the remaining salt and pepper and top with the lemon slices.

4. Brush a piece of parchment or wax paper with the remaining 1 teaspoon olive oil and place it, greased side-down, over the fish.

5. Bake 15 minutes, or until the fish is firm to the touch. Either serve directly from the dish, or carefully remove the fish fillets, make a bed of the vegetables on a platter and set the fish on top. Garnish with the parsley and basil before serving.

Red Snapper Goujonettes à la Barigoule

Goujonettes are a fun way to serve fish fillets. Referring to the tiny gudgeon fish, which is deep-fried whole (like smelts), the name *goujonettes* is actually a cut that is supposed to look like the little fish. Most recipes call for deep-frying the strips; however, poaching is also fairly common. Try to leave the skin on one side of the fillets. It helps hold the flesh together and adds flavor to the dish. This dish is also good at room temperature.

4 SERVINGS   22% CALORIES FROM FAT   278 CALORIES PER SERVING

> *¼ cup reduced-sodium chicken broth*
> *2 tablespoons finely chopped shallots*
> *6 sprigs of fresh thyme or ¼ teaspoon dried thyme leaves*
> *1 lemon, thinly sliced*
> *1½ pounds red snapper fillets, cut into 3-inch-long strips*
> *¼ cup white vermouth or dry white wine*
> *¼ teaspoon salt*
> *⅛ teaspoon freshly ground pepper*
> *Artichokes à la Barigoule with Tomatoes and Thyme (page 131)*

1. Preheat the oven to 400° F. Pour the chicken broth into an 8 × 11-inch baking dish. Scatter the shallots, thyme and lemon slices over the bottom of the dish. Arrange the fish fillet strips in a single layer. Pour the vermouth over the fish. Season with the salt and pepper.

2. Bake 10 to 12 minutes, or until the fish is opaque throughout. With a slotted spatula, transfer the strips to 4 plates, arranging them like the spokes of a wheel. Mound one-fourth of the artichokes in the center of each dish. Spoon some of the cooking liquid in the baking dish over the fish and serve at once.

Poached Salmon Trout with Aromatic Vegetables

If salmon trout are unavailable, golden trout or rainbow trout will work just fine. This dish can also be made with one small whole salmon (four to five pounds). Poached salmon trout are equally good hot or cold. Cold poached fish as part of a buffet table are always a treat. Serve with chilled Watercress Cream (page 93), or try it warm on a bed of wide noodles that have been tossed with heated Meaux Mustard Cream (page 88).

4 SERVINGS   30% CALORIES FROM FAT   360 CALORIES PER SERVING

1 tablespoon extra virgin olive oil
½ cup chopped onion
½ cup chopped carrot
½ cup chopped fennel
4 garlic cloves, finely chopped
2 lemons, cut into thin rounds
1 cup canned low-sodium chopped tomatoes, drained
1 bay leaf
4 sprigs of fresh thyme or ¼ teaspoon dried thyme leaves
4 sprigs of parsley
4 salmon trout (12 ounces each), cleaned and ready to cook
¼ teaspoon salt
¼ teaspoon freshly ground pepper
1 cup dry white wine
1 can (14½ ounces) reduced-sodium chicken broth
1 tablespoon chopped parsley
1 tablespoon chopped chives

1. Heat the olive oil in a large nonstick skillet. Add the onion, carrot, fennel and garlic, cover and cook over medium heat, stirring occasionally, until the vegetables are tender, 6 to 8 minutes.

2. Add the lemon slices, tomatoes, bay leaf, thyme and parsley sprigs. Place the fish over the vegetables. Season with the salt and pepper. Pour the wine and chicken broth over the fish.

3. Cover the skillet and bring the liquid to a boil. Reduce the heat to low and simmer 10 to 15 minutes, or until the fish is firm to the touch and opaque to the bone. Remove the fish to a serving plate and spoon the vegetables over the fish, using a slotted spoon.

4. Boil down the liquid remaining in the skillet until 1 cup remains. Pour this over the fish. Garnish with the chopped parsley and chives before serving.

—— *Roasted Monkfish "Gigot" with Thyme* ——

*G*igot is a term usually applied to a roast leg of lamb that has been stuck with cloves of garlic. Here the term is applied to a fish prepared with the same technique. The monkfish is stuck with garlic just like lamb, hence the French name for the dish: *gigot de lotte*. Monkfish, often known as "poor man's lobster," is sweet-tasting and firm. Try inserting the garlic slivers a few hours ahead of time so the flavor is better able to permeate the fish. Ratatouille is a natural accompaniment, but up north in Alsace, Savoy Cabbage Chiffonade (page 134) would complete the dish.

4 Servings   30% Calories from fat   191 Calories per serving

> *4 monkfish fillets, about ½ inch thick (6 ounces each)*
> *3 garlic cloves, cut into thin slivers*
> *1 tablespoon olive oil*
> *¼ teaspoon salt*
> *⅛ teaspoon freshly ground pepper*
> *8 sprigs of fresh thyme or ½ teaspoon dried thyme leaves*
> *2 lemons, thinly sliced*
> *¼ cup reduced-sodium chicken broth*
> *¼ cup white vermouth or dry white wine*

1. Preheat the oven to 400° F. With the point of a small paring knife, make shallow incisions all over the fish fillets and insert a garlic sliver into each cut.

2. Brush a small baking dish with the olive oil. Sprinkle half the salt, pepper, thyme and lemon slices over the bottom of the dish. Arrange the monkfish fillets in the dish in a single layer on top and season with the remaining salt, pepper, thyme and lemon slices.

3. Pour the chicken broth and wine over the fish and bake 12 to 15 minutes for every ½ inch of thickness, or until the fish is opaque to the center. Serve the fish with some of the pan juices spooned over the top.

Broiled Sole à l'Orange

Since orange juice is the main flavoring of this light dish, I recommend using freshly squeezed. The fish poaches in the juice, creating its own fragrant sauce, and the zucchini "noodles" make a lovely accompaniment.

4 Servings   24% Calories from fat   219 Calories per serving

1 medium shallot, finely chopped
4 sprigs of fresh thyme or ¼ teaspoon dried thyme leaves
¼ cup orange juice, preferably freshly squeezed
4 fillets of sole (6 ounces each)
2 tablespoons white vermouth or dry white wine
¼ teaspoon salt
⅛ teaspoon freshly ground pepper
Zucchini Noodles (recipe follows)

1. Preheat the oven to 400° F. Place the shallot, thyme and orange juice on the bottom of a small shallow baking dish just large enough to hold the fish in a single layer. Arrange the sole fillets in the dish and pour the vermouth over them. Season with the salt and pepper.

2. Bake the sole 8 to 12 minutes, until the fish is just white and opaque throughout.

3. To serve, arrange the zucchini noodles on a platter or divide them among 4 dinner plates. Set the fish fillets on top of the noodles, and spoon a couple of tablespoons of the pan juices over each piece of fish.

Zucchini Noodles

A mandoline or the julienne blade of a food processor must be used here to achieve the proper shape. For extra color appeal, use half green and half yellow zucchini. These "noodles" are a lovely accompaniment to delicate dishes, such as Broiled Sole à l'Orange. Tossed with pasta and some grated cheese, they can be transformed into a meatless main course.

4 SERVINGS   61% CALORIES FROM FAT   48 CALORIES PER SERVING

4 medium zucchini (about 1 pound)
1 tablespoon olive oil
1 garlic clove, finely chopped
Salt and freshly ground pepper
1 tablespoon chopped parsley
1 tablespoon finely shredded basil (or use 1 more tablespoon chopped parsley)

1. Scrub the zucchini well and trim off the ends. Using a mandoline or the julienne blade on a food processor, cut the zucchini into long, very thin strips.

2. In a large nonstick skillet, heat the olive oil over medium-high heat. Add the garlic and zucchini and cook, tossing often, until the zucchini is just tender, about 5 minutes.

3. Season with salt and pepper to taste. Add the parsley and basil, toss and serve.

Bouillabaisse

There's no question that this is the quintessential French fish stew. Here is a simple home-cooked version that is lighter than most chefs' interpretations. The technique for preparing bouillabaisse is to boil a variety of firm-fleshed fish and shellfish in an aromatic broth and ladle them into bowls over mashed boiled potato or toasted garlic bread. In this recipe, I've used seafood that is readily available and canned chicken broth rather than a complicated fish stock, so you can enjoy bouillabaisse any time you are in the mood. Rouille, a thick, garlicky, highly seasoned sauce, is served on the side to add flavor and spice to the dish.

6 Servings   20% Calories from fat   249 Calories per serving

1 orange
1 tablespoon extra virgin olive oil
1 cup diced (1/2-inch) onions
1 cup diced (1/2-inch) carrots
1 cup diced (1/2-inch) fennel bulb
2 tablespoons Pernod or other anise-flavored liquor
1 can (14 1/2 ounces) reduced-sodium chicken broth
3 garlic cloves, finely chopped
8 sprigs of fresh thyme or 1 teaspoon dried thyme leaves
8 sprigs of parsley
2 bay leaves
1 teaspoon fennel seeds
2 large tomatoes, peeled, seeded and coarsely chopped
1/2 teaspoon saffron threads, dissolved in 1/4 cup hot water
1/2 pound monkfish fillet, cut into 2-inch pieces
1/2 pound sea bass fillet, cut into 2-inch pieces
1 pound mussels, scrubbed and debearded
1/2 pound shrimp, shelled and deveined
4 small red potatoes, boiled until tender and peeled, or 4 slices of
    Toasted Garlic Bread (page 51)
Rouille, as accompaniment (page 105)

1. With a swivel-bladed vegetable peeler, remove the colored zest from the orange in long strips, taking care not to include any of the bitter white pith. Mince the orange zest.

2. In a stockpot or large flameproof casserole, heat the olive oil. Add the onions, carrots and fennel, cover and cook over medium-low heat, stirring occasionally, until the vegetables are tender, 10 to 15 minutes.

3. Uncover and raise the heat to medium. Pour in the Pernod and carefully ignite with a match. As soon as the flames subside, add the chicken broth, garlic, thyme, parsley, bay leaves, fennel seeds, orange zest and tomatoes. Simmer 10 minutes.

4. Add the dissolved saffron, the monkfish and sea bass to the broth. Cook over medium heat 5 minutes. Add the mussels, cover the pot and cook until they begin to open, 3 to 5 minutes. Add the shrimp and cook until they are pink and loosely curled, 2 or 3 minutes longer.

5. In each of 4 large soup bowls, either mash a potato roughly or set a piece of garlic toast. Ladle the bouillabaisse into the bowls, making sure everyone gets a sampling of the different seafood. Pass the rouille on the side.

Rouille

In this low-fat, no-cholesterol version of rouille, not a trace of oil or egg yolk is used, so you can spoon it on with abandon. Beware, though—it does have quite a kick.

MAKES ABOUT 1 CUP   6% CALORIES FROM FAT   13 CALORIES PER TABLESPOON

> *2 small red potatoes (about 2 ounces total)*
> *Roasted Red Peppers (page 34) or use 1 pound jarred roasted peppers,*
>   *well drained*
> *4 garlic cloves, crushed through a press*
> *¼ cup fresh lemon juice*
> *1 teaspoon cayenne pepper*
> *1 teaspoon paprika*
> *¼ teaspoon salt*

1. Peel the potatoes and cut them into quarters. Place in a small saucepan and add enough water to cover by 1 inch. Bring to a boil, reduce the heat to medium and cook until the potatoes are very soft, about 10 minutes. Drain.

2. In a blender or food processor, puree the roasted peppers smooth. Add the garlic, potatoes, lemon juice, cayenne, paprika and salt. Puree again until smooth.

3. If not serving within a couple of hours, cover and refrigerate the rouille for up to 2 days.

Bouillabaisse of Clams, Spinach, Potato and Saffron Broth

Most of us are familiar with bouillabaisse as the French fish stew, but the term, which roughly translates into "boiling hard without stopping," is applied to a whole family of similar soup/stew dishes. This particular bouillabaisse of clams comes from the Toulon area in the south of France. I have encountered bouillabaisse of spinach, potatoes and even chicken. All of these dishes are characteristically light in calories and very robust in flavor. Serve with spicy Rouille (recipe follows) on the side and some crusty garlic bread.

4 SERVINGS   20% CALORIES FROM FAT   301 CALORIES PER SERVING

1 tablespoon extra virgin olive oil
1 cup chopped onions
½ cup white vermouth or dry white wine
1 can (14½ ounces) reduced-sodium chicken broth
1 pound potatoes, peeled and cut into ½-inch pieces
2 garlic cloves, crushed through a press
6 sprigs of fresh thyme or ½ teaspoon dried thyme leaves
¼ teaspoon powdered saffron, diluted in ¼ cup warm water
48 littleneck, cherrystone or manilla clams, scrubbed
1 package (10 ounces) washed fresh spinach, trimmed and cut into ¼-inch-wide strips
1 teaspoon minced lemon zest

1. In a stockpot or large flameproof casserole, heat the olive oil. Add the onions, cover and cook over medium heat 2 minutes. Uncover and continue to cook, stirring occasionally, until soft and light golden in color, 3 to 5 minutes longer.

2. Pour in the vermouth and chicken broth and bring to a boil. Add the potatoes, garlic and thyme. Cook over medium heat 5 minutes; the potatoes should be slightly undercooked at this point.

3. Add the dissolved saffron and the clams. Raise the heat to high and cook at a rolling boil until the clams open, 5 to 10 minutes.

4. Toss in the spinach and lemon zest. Mix well until the spinach wilts. Ladle the soup into 4 bowls, dividing the clams evenly and discarding any that did not open.

Grilled Paillard of Swordfish with Harissa Sauce

A paillard is a thin cut, which cooks quickly. While the term often refers to meat, the same strategy works beautifully with fish. Ask your fishmonger to be sure the steaks are about ⅜ inch thick. Harissa is a spicy North African sauce that gives the fish a lift, but the paillards could just as well be served with a simple squeeze of fresh lemon.

4 Servings   36% Calories from fat   245 Calories per serving

4 thin swordfish steaks (about 6 ounces each)
2 teaspoons extra virgin olive oil
Salt and freshly ground pepper
Harissa Sauce (recipe follows)

1. Preheat the broiler or light a hot fire in a charcoal grill. Brush the fish with the olive oil and season lightly with salt and pepper.

2. Broil or grill the fish 8 to 10 minutes, without turning, until it is just opaque throughout. Spread about 1 tablespoon harissa sauce over each paillard and serve at once.

Harissa Sauce

Fiery harissa sauce, a popular Moroccan condiment, finds its way into all sorts of French dishes. It's a must with couscous and is excellent on grilled fish, chicken and even tossed with cooked vegetables like green beans, cauliflower and potatoes.

MAKES ABOUT 1 CUP   25% CALORIES FROM FAT   10 CALORIES PER TABLESPOON

> *1 ounce dried chili peppers*
> *3 garlic cloves, crushed through a press*
> *2 teaspoons paprika*
> *1 teaspoon ground caraway seed*
> *½ teaspoon ground cumin*
> *½ teaspoon ground coriander*
> *½ cup fresh lemon juice*
> *2 tablespoons chopped cilantro*
> *2 tablespoons reduced-sodium chicken broth*
> *½ teaspoon cayenne pepper*
> *¼ teaspoon salt*
> *¼ teaspoon freshly ground black pepper*

1. Place the dried chili peppers in a medium bowl and cover with boiling water. Let stand about 15 minutes, or until softened. Drain.

2. In a food processor or blender, puree the chili peppers until fairly smooth. Add all the remaining ingredients and blend well. Transfer to a covered container. Harissa will keep in the refrigerator for at least 1 month.

CHICKEN
AND
MEATS

"A chicken in every pot" isn't just politics to the French; it is the symbol of their very well-being. Chicken is the most popular meat in France. On the whole, the French consume far less meat than we Americans do. Traditionally, peasant dishes treat meat almost like a side dish, rather than the main event. For instance, the same recipe for coq au vin that would serve four in America, serves six in France.

In stews, braises and *daubes,* the main purpose of meat is to impart flavor to the dish. All of these long, slow-cooking processes make the most efficient use of inexpensive cuts. These dishes, known as *les plats mijoteux,* ("simmering dishes") are becoming less and less common, because just like in America, the average French family has less quality time to spend cooking. Roasts are reserved for special occasions and holidays. Quick-cooking thin cuts, such as chicken breasts or paillards of veal, pork or beef, are very popular because they are completely trimmed of all fat, deliver great flavor and are low in calories. Rabbit, which is also low in fat, is another popular option.

Except for the occasional Sunday roast, most French home cooks prefer the least complicated and healthiest ways to cook meat, as in grilling, "foil roasting" and braising. Paillards—thin, completely trimmed of all fat, cuts of meat that have been pounded to less than a ½ inch thickness—are best suited for quick cooking on a hot grill. A dish like Grilled Veal Paillard with Thyme cooks in 2 to 3 minutes. Another low-calorie technique is called cooking *en papillote* (in a package). Dishes, such as Foil-Steamed Chicken Breasts with Tarragon, Mushrooms and Wine, Chicken Breasts Niçoise and Roasted Rabbit with Tarragon Mustard Sauce, are all cooked with a minimum of fat and create their own delicious low-calorie sauce in their packets. For more information on this technique, see "Foil 'sauté' and foil 'roasting'" on page 17.

This chapter presents lightened versions of such classics as Coq au Vin, Cassoulet and Pot-au-Feu, which will make you wonder where all the calories went. For the Coq au Vin, I removed all of the skin and fat from the chicken and foil-roasted the blanched bacon and whole onions to attain that rich, caramelized flavor without all of the fat. Just enough flour was added before the wine to lightly thicken the stock. As a further slimming step, the coq au vin is completely cooked and cooled and the fat is skimmed off before reheating to serve.

In my lightened version of Cassoulet, the bean base, carefully cooked with tomatoes and aromatic vegetables, is what flavors the lean lamb and pork and the poultry sausage to a turn. For the Pot au Feu, I used beef tenderloin, totally trimmed of all fat, to poach in the flavorful broth for less than fifteen minutes. Sliced thin, this leanest of beef cuts is very low in calories and yet tender, without the long, slow cooking that a tougher, fattier piece of meat would have required. The result is traditional flavor without the fat.

Poulet Provençal

This light chicken sauté is always quick and easy to prepare. It can be cooked ahead and reheated. Serve with Zucchini Noodles (page 103) or with Provençal Lemon Herb Rice (page 161).

4 SERVINGS   30% CALORIES FROM FAT   259 CALORIES PER SERVING

1 tablespoon olive oil
1⅓ pounds skinless, boneless chicken breasts
1 medium onion, chopped
1 tablespoon finely chopped garlic
2 tablespoons dry white wine
4 sprigs of fresh thyme or ¼ teaspoon dried thyme leaves
1 can (14 ounces) low-salt chopped tomatoes, drained
¼ cup Mediterranean-style or other oil-cured black olives
¼ teaspoon salt
⅛ teaspoon freshly ground pepper
1 tablespoon chopped parsley
1 tablespoon finely shredded basil leaves (or add 1 more tablespoon chopped parsley)

1. In a large nonstick skillet, heat 1 teaspoon of the olive oil. Add the chicken and cook over medium-high heat, turning once, until golden on both sides, about 5 minutes. Remove the chicken from the pan and set aside.

2. In the same pan, heat the remaining 2 teaspoons olive oil. Add the onion and garlic, cover and cook over medium heat 2 minutes. Uncover and cook, stirring occasionally, until tender, about 3 minutes longer.

3. Add the wine, raise the heat to high and boil until reduced to a syrup, about 3 minutes. Add the thyme, tomatoes, olives, chicken breasts and any cooking juices that may have accumulated on the plate. Simmer over medium-low heat 15 minutes, or until the chicken is tender.

4. Season with the salt and pepper and garnish with the parsley and basil before serving.

Coq au vin is a beloved dish on both sides of the Atlantic. In this recipe, roasting the onions, carrots and bacon in foil brings out all of their luscious caramelized flavor without added fat. I prefer to make this dish ahead of time so that it can cool down and I can skim the fat off of the top. The waiting period also allows the flavors to develop. Serve with plain boiled potatoes.

4 SERVINGS   30% CALORIES FROM FAT   360 CALORIES PER SERVING

1 slice of lean bacon, cut into ¼-inch dice
1 pound small, white boiling onions (about 1 inch in diameter), peeled
3 or 4 medium carrots (½ pound), peeled and cut into ½-inch dice
6 garlic cloves
1 tablespoon olive oil
1 chicken (3 to 3½ pounds), skinned and cut into 8 serving pieces
1 bay leaf
3 sprigs of parsley
3 sprigs of fresh thyme or ¼ teaspoon dried thyme leaves
¼ teaspoon salt
¼ teaspoon freshly ground pepper
2 tablespoons flour
2 cups dry white wine
1 cup reduced-sodium chicken broth
1 tablespoon chopped parsley

1. Preheat the oven to 400° F. Bring a small saucepan of water to a boil. Add the bacon and cook 30 seconds. Drain and rinse briefly under running water. Pat dry on a paper towel.

2. Line an 8- or 9-inch square baking dish with foil, leaving plenty of overlap. Mix the bacon, onions, carrots, garlic and olive oil together and spread out on the foil. Seal the foil tightly and bake 45 minutes, or until the onions are just tender.

3. Empty the contents of the foil into a large flameproof casserole. Add the chicken, bay leaf, parsley, thyme, salt and pepper. Sprinkle the flour over the chicken pieces and stir until the white disappears. Add the wine and chicken broth.

4. Bring to a boil over high heat. Reduce heat to low, cover tightly and simmer 1½ hours, or until the chicken is very tender. Let cool completely, then refrigerate for several hours or overnight.

5. Before serving, skim off all the fat that solidifies on top of the sauce. Reheat the coq au vin over medium heat. Serve garnished with the chopped parsley.

Grilled Chicken "Diable"

Sauce "diable"—devil sauce—is a favorite French barbecue sauce. This naturally low-calorie combination is really easy to prepare and is delicious on steak, roasted rabbit or on fish like swordfish or halibut.

4 SERVINGS   18% CALORIES FROM FAT   149 CALORIES PER SERVING

> *1 teaspoon olive oil*
> *2 tablespoons finely chopped shallots*
> *1 tablespoon Dijon mustard*
> *¼ teaspoon cayenne pepper, or more to taste*
> *2 teaspoons Worcestershire sauce*
> *½ cup reduced-sodium chicken broth*
> *1 tablespoon finely chopped parsley*
> *4 skinless, boneless chicken breast halves (4 ounces each)*

1. Preheat the broiler and set the rack 5 to 6 inches below the heat source. Brush a 12-inch gratin or 8 × 11-inch flameproof baking dish with the olive oil.

2. In a medium bowl, combine the shallots, mustard, cayenne, Worcestershire, chicken broth and parsley. Stir until well blended. Add the chicken breasts and turn until they are well coated.

3. Place the chicken breasts in the baking dish in a single layer. Scrape the contents of the bowl over them. Broil 5 to 8 minutes, without turning, until the chicken is no longer pink in the center. Serve hot or at room temperature.

Chicken Breasts Niçoise

Quick, easy and light are what I go for when entertaining on a weekday work night. I can prepare this dish the night before and refrigerate it until I'm ready to pop it in the oven. Serve with roasted potatoes and steamed asparagus or green beans.

4 SERVINGS   30% CALORIES FROM FAT   216 CALORIES PER SERVING

4 skinless, boneless chicken breast halves (4 ounces each)
1 tablespoon extra virgin olive oil
2 garlic cloves, finely chopped
½ cup thinly sliced red onion
1 large green bell pepper, thinly sliced
4 plum tomatoes, peeled, seeded and chopped
8 sprigs of fresh thyme or ½ teaspoon dried thyme leaves
¼ teaspoon salt
⅛ teaspoon freshly ground pepper
4 (2-inch) pieces of orange zest
16 Niçoise or other oil-cured black olives
¼ cup white vermouth or dry white wine
¼ cup reduced-sodium chicken broth

1. Preheat the oven to 400° F. Trim any fat or gristle from the chicken.

2. Line a 9-inch square baking dish with a sheet of aluminum foil, leaving plenty of overlap. Brush the olive oil over the foil. Layer the garlic, onion, pepper and tomatoes evenly in the dish.

3. Arrange the chicken on top of the vegetables in a single layer. Season with the thyme, salt and pepper. Place a strip of orange zest on top of each chicken breast. Scatter the olives over the chicken. Pour the wine and chicken broth over all. Fold up the edges of the foil and crimp tightly to seal, using another sheet of foil, if necessary.

4. Bake 15 to 20 minutes, or until the chicken is no longer pink in the center. To serve, slide the chicken and vegetables off the foil onto a plate. Spoon some of the pan juices over the chicken.

Poulet Sauté Chasseur

Poulet chasseur, hunter-style chicken, is even better when prepared ahead of time and reheated. When the dish is allowed to cool down completely and the fat is skimmed off, it becomes lighter and more intensely flavored. Serve with plain boiled potatoes or noodles.

4 SERVINGS   25% CALORIES FROM FAT   194 CALORIES PER SERVING

> *1 tablespoon olive oil*
> *4 skinless, boneless chicken breast halves (4 ounces each)*
> *½ cup finely diced carrots*
> *½ cup finely diced onions*
> *½ cup dry red wine*
> *½ cup canned low-salt chopped tomatoes, drained*
> *½ cup reduced-sodium chicken broth*
> *½ pound white mushrooms, sliced*
> *¼ teaspoon salt*
> *⅛ teaspoon freshly ground pepper*
> *1 tablespoon finely chopped parsley*

1. In a large nonstick skillet, heat 1 teaspoon of the olive oil. Add the chicken and cook over medium-high heat, turning once, until golden brown on both sides, about 5 minutes. Remove the chicken from the pan and set aside.

2. In the same pan, add the remaining 2 teaspoons olive oil, the carrots and onions. Press a sheet of foil right down on the vegetables and cook over medium heat, stirring once or twice, until the carrots are tender and the onion is lightly colored, about 5 minutes.

3. Add the wine, raise the heat to high and boil until reduced to a syrup, 3 to 4 minutes. Add the tomatoes, chicken broth, mushrooms, chicken breasts and any cooking juices that may have accumulated on the plate. Simmer over medium-low heat 15 minutes, or until the chicken is tender.

4. Season with the salt and pepper and garnish with the parsley before serving.

Poulet Sauté au Vinaigre

Au vinaigre is a delicious, naturally light, sweet and sour sauce that goes well with grilled duck breasts, pork and veal, as well as with pan-roasted salmon (page 87) or on grilled halibut or swordfish. Serve with Zucchini Noodles (page 103) or steamed rice.

4 SERVINGS   25% CALORIES FROM FAT   191 CALORIES PER SERVING

1 tablespoon olive oil
4 skinless, boneless chicken breast halves (4 ounces each)
½ cup finely diced carrots
½ cup finely diced onions
1 teaspoon finely chopped garlic
1 tablespoon sherry wine vinegar or balsamic vinegar
1 tablespoon tomato paste
1 teaspoon sugar
2 tablespoons green peppercorns (packed in brine), drained
1 cup reduced-sodium chicken broth
⅛ teaspoon salt
1 tablespoon finely chopped parsley

1. In a large nonstick skillet, heat 1 teaspoon of the olive oil. Add the chicken and cook over medium-high heat, turning once, until golden brown on both sides, about 5 minutes. Remove the chicken from the pan and set aside.

2. In the same pan, heat the remaining 2 teaspoons olive oil, the carrots, onions and garlic. Press a sheet of aluminum foil right down on the vegetables and cook over medium heat, stirring once or twice, until the carrots are tender and the onion is lightly colored, about 5 minutes.

3. Add the vinegar, turn the heat to high and cook 1 minute, or until reduced to a syrup. Add the tomato paste, sugar, peppercorns, chicken broth, chicken breasts and any cooking juices that may have accumulated on the plate. Simmer over medium-low heat 15 minutes, or until the chicken is tender.

4. Season with the salt and garnish with the parsley before serving.

Chicken in a Pot Grandmère

This is a simple dish, just like grandmother used to make, conjuring up all sorts of feelings of well-being. With tender chicken, broth and simple vegetables, the dish is a naturally light one, but removing the skin from the chicken before cooking reduces the fat and calories tremendously.

4 SERVINGS   28% CALORIES FROM FAT   400 CALORIES PER SERVING

> 1 strip of bacon, cut into ¼-inch dice
> 1 tablespoon olive oil
> 2 medium onions, thickly sliced
> 4 medium carrots (½ pound), peeled and thickly sliced
> 1 chicken (3 pounds), skinned and cut into 8 serving pieces
> 1 bay leaf
> 3 sprigs of parsley
> 3 sprigs of fresh thyme or ¼ teaspoon dried thyme leaves
> 1 pound small red potatoes, scrubbed and halved if larger than 2 inches
>   in diameter
> 2 cans (14½ ounces each) reduced-sodium chicken broth
> ¼ teaspoon freshly ground pepper
> 1 tablespoon chopped parsley

1. Bring a small saucepan of water to a boil. Add the bacon and cook 30 seconds. Drain and rinse briefly under running water. Pat dry on a paper towel.

2. In a large, heavy stew pot with a lid, heat the olive oil and add the bacon, onions and carrots. Press a sheet of aluminum foil right down on the vegetables and cook over medium heat, stirring once or twice, until the onions are golden and the carrots are just tender, about 10 minutes.

3. Add the chicken pieces, bay leaf, parsley sprigs, thyme, potatoes, chicken broth and pepper. Bring to a boil over medium-high heat. Reduce the heat to low, cover and simmer 1½ hours. Serve garnished with the chopped parsley.

— *Pan-Roasted Duck Breasts à L'Orange With* — *Shallot Confit*

Duck is a very rich and flavorful meat, and surprisingly calorically afford- able, if the skin and all visible fat are removed before cooking. In this recipe, duck breasts are roasted on a bed of shallot confit and thyme. The sauce is an *à la minute* mélange of vinegar, chicken broth, orange zest and orange juice. Its body comes from the shallot confit. This cooking method also suits pork or even a thick piece of fresh tuna. Serve with Zucchini Noodles (page 103) or with Spinach with Parmesan Cheese and Pine Nuts (page 145).

4 Servings   34% Calories from fat   281 Calories per serving

> 1 orange
> 1 tablespoon extra virgin olive oil
> 1 pound shallots, peeled and halved
> 4 sprigs of fresh thyme or ¼ teaspoon dried thyme leaves
> 1 tablespoon sherry wine vinegar or balsamic vinegar
> 1 pound boneless, fresh or thawed frozen skinless duck breasts, trimmed
>   of all fat
> ½ cup reduced-sodium chicken broth
> ½ cup orange juice
> ¼ teaspoon salt
> ⅛ teaspoon freshly ground pepper

1. Preheat the oven to 400° F. With a zester, remove the zest from the or- ange in thin strips. Or use a swivel-bladed vegetable peeler to take off larger pieces and cut those into fine strips. Bring a small saucepan of water to a boil. Add the orange zest and cook 30 seconds; drain. Reserve the orange for the juice used in step 6.

2. Line an 8 × 11-inch baking pan or a 12-inch gratin with a sheet of foil, leaving plenty of overlap. Combine 2 teaspoons of the olive oil, the shallots, thyme and the vinegar in the pan. Seal the foil edges to form a packet. Bake 30 to 40 minutes, or until the shallots are very tender. Set the shallot confit aside.

3. Brush a large nonstick skillet with an ovenproof handle or a flameproof gratin dish with the remaining olive oil. Set over high heat. Add the duck breasts and cook until they are nicely golden on the bottom, 2 to 3 minutes. Set the duck breasts aside on a plate.

4. Add the shallot confit to the skillet and reheat over medium heat, stirring, until hot, about 3 minutes. Place the duck breasts, browned side-up, on top of the shallot confit.

5. Transfer to the oven and roast the duck breasts 8 minutes for rare, 10 minutes for medium and 15 minutes for well done. When the meat is done, remove it to a dish and cover with foil to keep warm.

6. Add the orange zest, chicken broth and orange juice to the shallot confit in the skillet. Boil over high heat or until the liquid is reduced by half, about 5 minutes. Season with salt and pepper to taste, pour over the duck breasts and serve at once.

— *Foil-Steamed Chicken Breasts with Tarragon,* — *Mushrooms and Wine*

Cooking *en papillote* seals in the juices, rendering a delicious sauce. All this with a minimum of calories and easy cleanup, too.

4 Servings   26% Calories from fat   188 Calories per serving

> *1 tablespoon olive oil*
> *4 large shallots, thinly sliced*
> *1 pound skinless, boneless chicken breasts*
> *¼ cup dry white wine*
> *½ pound mushrooms, thinly sliced*
> *8 sprigs of fresh tarragon or ½ teaspoon dried tarragon leaves*
> *¼ teaspoon salt*
> *⅛ teaspoon freshly ground pepper*

1. Preheat the oven to 400° F. Line a 9-inch square baking dish with aluminum foil, leaving about 4 inches extra on two sides. Brush the olive oil over the foil on the bottom of the dish and sprinkle on the shallots. Arrange the chicken breasts in a single layer over the shallots.

2. Pour the wine over the chicken, layer the mushrooms on top and season with the tarragon, salt and pepper. Fold up the edges of the foil and crimp to seal, using another sheet of foil if necessary.

3. Bake 15 minutes, or until the chicken is no longer pink inside. To serve, remove the chicken with a spatula and pour the sauce and mushrooms back over it.

Pot-au-Feu—Poached Beef, Vegetables and Broth

Pot-au-feu—the famous boiled dinner—is one of the glories of French home cooking. Meats and vegetables, simple and unadulterated, are slow cooked. *Pot-au-feu* is intentionally bland, the idea being that each diner seasons the meat and vegetables to his or her own taste with a selection of traditional condiments.

Traditionally the cuts of meat employed in *pot-au-feu* are tough and fatty; consequently, the long, slow cooking process makes the most out of economical cuts. In this recipe, we are trying to get the most flavor and the least fat out of the meat we consume. I've replaced those fatty cuts of meat with trimmed beef tenderloin, which is very lean, tender and flavorful when quickly poached. Best of all, it cooks in less than 15 minutes.

6 SERVINGS   28% CALORIES FROM FAT   340 CALORIES PER SERVING

1 pound carrots, peeled and cut into 1-inch chunks
1 pound onions, peeled and quartered
2 medium parsnips, peeled and cut into 1-inch chunks
2 large white turnips, peeled and cut into 1-inch chunks
6 garlic cloves
4 cans (14½ ounces each) reduced-sodium chicken broth
6 cloves
1 bay leaf
4 sprigs of fresh thyme
4 sprigs of parsley
10 peppercorns
3 medium leeks, trimmed, split, cleaned and tied with string
1 small Savoy cabbage (1 pound), trimmed, cored and quartered
1½ pounds trimmed beef tenderloin roast, tied
Coarse salt, cornichons (tiny French gherkin pickles) and Sauce au Raifort (recipe follows), as accompaniments

1. In a large pot, combine the carrots, onions, parsnips, turnips and garlic with the chicken broth and 2 cups of water. Add the cloves, bay leaf, thyme, parsley and peppercorns. Bring to a boil over high heat. Cover, reduce the heat to medium-low and simmer 15 minutes.

2. Add the leeks and simmer 15 minutes. Add the cabbage and simmer 30 minutes. When all of the vegetables are tender, use a slotted spoon or skimmer to remove them to a serving platter. Cover with foil to keep warm (remove the string from the leeks).

3. Immerse the beef tenderloin into the broth. (Make sure the meat is completely submerged.) Simmer 8 minutes for rare, 10 minutes for medium rare or 15 minutes for well done.

4. Remove the meat from the broth and slice thinly. Serve the meat slices on top of the vegetables, moistened with some of the broth. Serve some of the broth in small bowls or cups on the side to eat as soup. Pass bowls of coarse salt, cornichons and sauce au raifort on the side.

Sauce au Raifort

MAKES ABOUT 1 CUP   1% CALORIES FROM FAT   7 CALORIES PER TABLESPOON

¼ cup prepared white horseradish
¾ cup nonfat plain yogurt

In a small bowl, combine the horseradish and yogurt. Stir until well blended. Cover and refrigerate until serving time.

Steak au Poivre

This lightened version of au poivre is achieved without butter or cream. I've chosen tenderloin steaks, or *filet mignon,* because they are one of the leanest and yet most tender cuts of beef, which lend themselves to this quick pan-frying method.

4 SERVINGS   49% CALORIES FROM FAT   228 CALORIES PER SERVING

> 2 teaspoons olive oil
> 4 tenderloin steaks (4 ounces each), trimmed of all fat and pounded to
>   ½ inch thickness
> 1 tablespoon Cognac or brandy
> 1 tablespoon finely chopped shallot
> 2 tablespoons green peppercorns (packed in brine), drained
> 1 teaspoon Dijon mustard
> 1 cup reduced-sodium chicken broth

1. In a large nonstick skillet, heat the olive oil over medium-high heat until hot. Add the steaks and cook, flipping them once midway during cooking, 5 minutes for rare, 8 to 10 minutes for medium and 15 minutes for well done. Remove the steaks to a platter and cover with foil to keep warm while finishing the sauce.

2. Add the Cognac and shallot to the skillet (be careful to avert your face in case the liquor flames up). Boil 1 minute over high heat. Add the green peppercorns, mustard and chicken broth. Bring to a boil and cook over high heat until reduced by half to about ½ cup, 3 or 4 minutes.

3. Pour the sauce over the steaks and serve at once.

Cassoulet of White Beans, Lamb, Pork and Sausage

Light cassoulet might come as a surprise to many. But, yes, it can be done! At the very heart of this dish is the succulence of the beans; if that base is not flavorful, the dish will miss. Add meats as a condiment rather than as a main feature, and you're starting to get somewhere. In this version, the duck or goose fat and confit has been left out. In their stead is lean lamb, pork and poultry sausages—still traditional, but with a nod to the waistline. For entertaining, it's nice to know that this dish reheats well.

8 Servings   24% Calories from fat   310 Calories per serving

White Beans Cassoulet Style (page 165), prepared through step 4
10 ounces well-trimmed boneless pork loin, cut into 1-inch cubes
10 ounces well-trimmed boneless leg of lamb, cut into 1-inch cubes
½ pound smoked chicken or turkey sausages, cut into 2-inch pieces
1 tablespoon chopped parsley

1. Preheat the oven to 375° F. After completing step 4 of the bean recipe, add the pork and lamb. Bring to a boil on top of the stove. Cover and transfer to the oven. Bake 1 hour.

2. Add the sausages and a little more broth or water if the cassoulet appears a bit dry. Cover and continue baking 1 hour longer, or until the meats and beans are meltingly tender.

3. Serve with a sprinkling of parsley on top.

Roasted Leg of Lamb with Olives

Leg of lamb, or *gigot*, as the French call it, was always one of my favorite Sunday meals. Serve this savory meat with Roasted Potato Slices with Garlic and Herbs (page 139) and steamed green beans.

6 SERVINGS   42% CALORIES FROM FAT   293 CALORIES PER SERVING

3 pounds boneless leg of lamb, trimmed of all fat
2 garlic cloves, thinly sliced
1 tablespoon olive oil
4 sprigs of fresh thyme or ¼ teaspoon dried thyme leaves
½ teaspoon salt
¼ teaspoon freshly ground pepper
About ½ cup reduced-sodium chicken broth
1 tablespoon Pernod or other pastis liquor
2 plum tomatoes, peeled, seeded and chopped
16 oil-cured black olives
1 tablespoon chopped parsley

1. Preheat the oven to 400° F. Make small incisions all over the lamb and insert the garlic. Rub the olive oil into the lamb and season with the thyme, salt and pepper. Place the meat in a small, flameproof roasting pan.

2. Roast the lamb, basting with the chicken broth every 10 or 15 minutes, 15 minutes per pound for rare, 20 minutes per pound for medium-rare and 25 to 30 minutes per pound for well done. Remove the roast to a cutting board and let stand 10 minutes before slicing.

3. Tilt the roasting pan and skim off as much fat as you can from the pan juices. Heat the roasting pan on top of the stove. Add the Pernod and carefully ignite with a match. As soon as the flames subside, add the tomatoes, olives and parsley. Cook for 1 to 2 minutes, scraping up all the brown bits from the bottom of the pan. Season with additional salt and pepper to taste.

4. Carve the lamb into thin slices and spoon the sauce with the tomatoes and olives over the meat.

Roasted Pork Loin with Fennel, Garlic and Tomato

Pork is an excellent meat, low in calories and so flavorful. This roast is also delicious served cold, carved into thin slices.

4 SERVINGS   43% CALORIES FROM FAT   341 CALORIES PER SERVING

2 pounds center-cut boneless pork loin roast, trimmed of all fat
2 garlic cloves, thinly sliced
1 tablespoon olive oil
1 medium fennel bulb, thinly sliced
1 small onion, thinly sliced
6 sprigs of fresh thyme or ½ teaspoon dried thyme leaves
¼ teaspoon salt
¼ teaspoon freshly ground pepper
1 cup reduced-sodium chicken broth, warmed
1 can (14 ounces) low-salt chopped tomatoes, drained

1. Preheat the oven to 400° F. Make small incisions all over the pork roast and insert the garlic slices. Rub the olive oil into the pork.

2. In a small roasting pan, layer the fennel, onion and thyme on the bottom and place the pork on top. Season the roast with the salt and pepper.

3. Roast the pork, turning the meat and basting with the broth every 15 minutes, 1 hour. Remove the pork to a cutting board and let it rest for 10 minutes before slicing.

4. Scrape all of the roasting pan contents into a small nonreactive saucepan. Add any remaining broth and boil down to ½ cup. Add the tomatoes and simmer 5 minutes longer. Season with additional salt and pepper to taste. Spoon the sauce over the sliced pork and serve.

Veal Stew Merango

Serve veal merango over plain noodles or with boiled potatoes. It's the kind of dish that is better the following day, so feel free to make it in advance.

4 SERVINGS   28% CALORIES FROM FAT   365 CALORIES PER SERVING

1 tablespoon plus 1 teaspoon olive oil
1 medium onion, cut into ½-inch dice
2 pounds veal stew meat, trimmed of all fat and cut into 2-inch pieces
½ cup dry white wine
1 tablespoon flour
3 sprigs of parsley
3 sprigs of fresh thyme or ¼ teaspoon dried thyme leaves
1 bay leaf
2 (2-inch) strips of lemon zest
3 garlic cloves, minced
1 can (14 ounces) low-salt chopped tomatoes, drained
1½ cups reduced-sodium chicken broth
¼ teaspoon salt
⅛ teaspoon freshly ground pepper
1 pound mushrooms, quartered
1 tablespoon chopped parsley

1. In a large nonstick skillet, heat 2 teaspoons of the olive oil. Add the onion, cover and cook over medium heat 2 minutes. Uncover and continue to cook until tender and lightly colored, about 3 minutes longer. Scrape the onion into a 2½- to 3-quart stew pot or flameproof casserole.

2. In the same skillet, heat the remaining 2 teaspoons olive oil. Add the veal and cook over medium-high heat, turning, until lightly browned, 5 to 7 minutes. Add the meat to the stew pot.

3. Pour the wine into the skillet and bring to a boil over high heat, scraping up the browned bits from the bottom of the pan with a spatula. Pour the wine over the veal.

4. Sprinkle the flour over the meat and stir until the white disappears. Add the sprigs of parsley, the thyme, bay leaf, lemon zest, garlic, tomatoes, chicken broth, salt and pepper. Bring to a boil over medium-high heat. Lower the heat to medium-low, cover and simmer 45 minutes, or until the meat is tender.

5. Add the mushrooms and simmer 15 minutes longer. Serve garnished with the chopped parsley.

Grilled Veal Paillard with Thyme

Paillard means "thin straw mat" in French. The term is loosely applied to thin cuts of meat, fish and poultry. *Paillards* make a lot of sense to those of us who still want all the flavor of meat but not the huge portions. Serve this dish with Roasted Potato Slices with Garlic and Herbs (page 139) and Spinach with Lemon Confit and Olives (page 144).

4 SERVINGS   29% CALORIES FROM FAT   174 CALORIES PER SERVING

> *1 pound veal leg, cut into 4 thin cutlets (scallopine)*
> *1 tablespoon extra virgin olive oil*
> *Salt and freshly ground pepper*
> *1 cup tomato sauce*
> *2 teaspoons fresh thyme leaves or ½ teaspoon dried*
> *2 tablespoons fresh orange juice*

1. Preheat the broiler or light a hot fire in a charcoal grill.

2. Rub the veal with the extra virgin olive oil and season with salt and pepper.

3. Broil or grill the veal about 4 inches from the heat, 2 to 3 minutes on each side.

4. Spoon about ¼ cup of the tomato sauce on each plate and place the cooked veal on top. Sprinkle with the thyme and orange juice before serving.

Roasted Rabbit with Tarragon Mustard Sauce

Rabbit, which is quite popular in French country cooking, is a mild-flavored meat that is lean and naturally low in calories. In this version of the classic *lapin à la moutarde* (rabbit with mustard), nonfat yogurt replaces the rich French *crème fraîche*. The effect, however, is no less succulent. This treatment works equally well for chicken, too. Serve with plain noodles and Zucchini-Carrot Julienne with Garlic and Herbs (page 151).

4 Servings   42% Calories from fat   395 Calories per serving

1 rabbit (3 pounds), cut into 8 serving pieces
2 teaspoons olive oil
Salt and freshly ground pepper
2 tablespoons Dijon mustard
¼ cup nonfat plain yogurt
2 shallots, thinly sliced
2 teaspoons finely chopped garlic
2 teaspoons fresh tarragon leaves or ½ teaspoon dried

1. Preheat the oven to 400° F. Rub the rabbit with the olive oil and season lightly with salt and pepper. Line a shallow baking dish with aluminum foil, allowing several inches of overlap, and place the rabbit pieces in the center.

2. In a small bowl, combine the Dijon mustard, yogurt, shallots, garlic and tarragon. Mix together until well blended.

3. Pour the mustard-yogurt sauce over the rabbit and toss the pieces around until each is well coated. Place another sheet of foil on top and crimp the edges of the 2 sheets together to seal. Bake 1½ hours.

Chapter Six

VEGETABLES

Vegetables are the heart and soul of French country cuisine. For centuries, peasants survived on what they could grow from the ground; meat was really a condiment in cooking. Tending *le potager,* or vegetable garden, is still a national pastime. Garden plots dot the countryside and surround the outer skirts of urban areas, forming square patches of color like a Cézanne painting. In the open-air markets, picture-perfect vegetables, lovingly displayed, glisten like jewels. Whether in a tiny village or in a large city, the marketplace is a treat to the senses, and always an inspiration to the cook.

Now that notion of eating lots of healthful vegetables with just a little meat, fish or cheese has come full circle. Serious vegetable gardening is catching on in America, too. And supermarkets all over the country focus on acquiring the freshest and most beautiful produce. We are relearning to appreciate what the good earth bears. French peasants focused on vegetables because of economics; today we focus on vegetables because of health. Naturally high in complex carbohydrates, fiber, vitamins and minerals, vegetables are the wise path to follow for healthy, low-fat eating.

This chapter contains the essence of French country vegetable cookery. Most of the dishes are so naturally low in calories that little or nothing was done to lighten them. Many of these dishes have multiple uses as appetizers, side dishes or main courses.

One of my favorite methods to use on vegetables is "foil roasting." Vegetables, such as Carrots Provençal with Sweet Vermouth and Fennel, Tomatoes Provençal, Roasted Zucchini Fans with Thyme, Roasted Onion Confit and Roasted Potato Slices with Garlic and Herbs, are prepared with a minimum of fat. When the vegetables "roast" in the foil, they literally absorb the seasonings, and their flavors become intense. From the sunny South of France comes a selection of *petits farcis* ("little stuffed vegetables"): Zucchini Barquettes Filled with Olives, Onion and Tomato and Baked Peppers Stuffed with Rice, Sausage and Tomatoes. These practical small dishes are excellent as appetizers, or first courses or a light lunch.

For more substantial preparations, braises, such as Artichokes à la Barigoule with Tomatoes and Thyme, Green Beans Gourmandise with Tomato, Onion and Garlic and Savoy Cabbage Chiffonade, can serve as a side dish, chilled as an appetizer or as a light lunch. For the potato lover, there are comforting—and, yes, low-in-calorie dishes such as Stuffed Baked Potatoes Cinderella, Potato Mousseline with Red and White Carrots and Potatoes Mashed with Spinach, Garlic and Cheese. Also included is a duo of baked gratins—Potato, Onion and Tomato Gratin and Vegetable Gratin with Tomatoes, Rice and Parmesan Cheese. Either of these make a wonderful side dish or light entree.

Artichokes à la Barigoule with Tomatoes and Thyme

Barigoule is Provençal dialect for "thyme" (*farigoule*). Artichokes are a luscious exceptionally low-calorie treat. This dish can be served cold as an appetizer or warm as a side dish for fish and meats, or tossed with pasta. Artichokes à la barigoule is best prepared ahead of time. Try to find the smallest, most tender artichokes for this dish.

4 SERVINGS   30% CALORIES FROM FAT   112 CALORIES PER SERVING

> 8 small Italian artichokes (about 1 pound) (see Note)
> 1 tablespoon lemon juice
> 1 tablespoon olive oil
> 1 large carrot, cut into ¼-inch dice
> 1 medium onion, cut into ¼-inch dice
> 1 garlic clove, thinly sliced
> 1 cup dry white wine
> 1 can (14½ ounces) reduced-sodium chicken broth
> 3 plum tomatoes, peeled, seeded and chopped
> 8 sprigs of fresh thyme or ½ teaspoon dried thyme leaves
> 1 bay leaf
> Salt and freshly ground pepper

1. Cut off the artichoke stems and trim the outer tough leaves from the artichokes. Cut each in half or into quarters, depending on the size. Trim out the hairy choke. Put the artichokes in a medium bowl, sprinkle them with the lemon juice and toss.

2. In a large nonstick skillet, heat the olive oil. Add the artichokes, carrot, onion and garlic. Cover and cook over medium heat, stirring from time to time, 15 minutes, or until the vegetables begin to soften.

3. Add the wine, chicken broth, tomatoes, thyme, bay leaf and 2 cups of water. Simmer, uncovered, 45 minutes to 1 hour, or until the artichokes are completely tender. Season with salt and pepper to taste and serve hot or cold.

NOTE *If tiny Italian artichokes are not available in your market, use globe artichokes and cut them lengthwise into 8 wedges each.*

Garlic Confit

If you enjoy garlic, then *confit d'ail* is for you. Long, slow cooking produces a smooth, mild-flavored and mellow garlic to be spread on grilled bread or added to pasta, rice, potatoes or vegetables. Be sure to use the fragrant oil the confit is covered with for salads or in cooking. Each teaspoon of the oil will cost you 40 calories.

ABOUT 16 SERVINGS   29% CALORIES FROM FAT   26 CALORIES PER SERVING

> *2 large heads of garlic (½ pound)*
> *2 cups olive oil*
> *¼ teaspoon dried thyme leaves*
> *1 bay leaf*
> *6 whole peppercorns*

1. Separate the cloves of garlic, peel them and place them in a small saucepan. Add the olive oil, thyme, bay leaf and peppercorns.

2. Bring to a simmer over medium heat. Reduce the heat to low and simmer gently, uncovered, 45 to 60 minutes, or until the garlic is very tender.

3. Let the confit cool completely before storing the garlic with the oil in a covered jar. To serve, remove the cloves as needed and drain on paper towels; allow 4 per serving.

Sweet Garlic Puree

Use sweet garlic puree instead of butter on bread, in vegetables, in pasta or as a thickener in soups and sauces. You can feel free to spread this versatile puree on just about anything as it is really light and low in calories, but high in flavor.

MAKES ABOUT 1 CUP   7% CALORIES FROM FAT   21 CALORIES PER SERVING

3 heads of garlic (½ pound), separated into cloves, skins on
1 can (14½ ounces) reduced-sodium chicken broth

1. In a medium saucepan, combine the garlic, chicken broth and 2 cups of water. Bring to a boil over high heat. Reduce the heat and simmer about 1 hour, or until almost all of the cooking liquid has evaporated.

2. Press the garlic through a fine-mesh sieve or use a food mill or potato ricer, pushing the garlic into a small bowl and leaving the skins behind.

3. Store in a small airtight container or covered jar in the refrigerator for up to 2 weeks.

Savoy Cabbage Chiffonade

Savoy cabbage, the pale, crinkly kind, is a very fine vegetable, milder in flavor and more delicate in texture than the ordinary green kind. It is extremely low in calories and rich in nutrients, such as vitamin C. This preparation goes well with pork, chicken, fish or seafood. If Savoy cabbage is unavailable, Napa cabbage can be substituted.

8 Servings   47% Calories from fat   60 Calories per serving

> *1 slice of lean bacon, cut into ¼-inch dice*
> *1 tablespoon olive oil*
> *2 medium carrots, peeled and chopped*
> *1 medium onion, chopped*
> *1 small head of Savoy cabbage (1 pound), cut into ¼-inch-wide strips*
> *1 can (14½ ounces) reduced-sodium chicken broth*
> *Salt and freshly ground pepper*

1. Bring a small saucepan of water to a boil. Add the bacon and cook 30 seconds. Drain and rinse briefly under running water. Pat dry on a paper towel.

2. In a large nonstick skillet or flameproof casserole, heat the olive oil. Add the bacon, carrots and onion. Press a sheet of aluminum foil right down on the vegetables and cook over medium heat, stirring occasionally, until the carrots are tender and the onion is golden, 7 to 10 minutes.

3. Add the cabbage and chicken broth, reduce the heat to medium-low and cook, covered, until the cabbage is tender, 15 to 20 minutes.

4. Season with salt and pepper to taste and serve hot.

— *Carrots Provençal with Sweet Vermouth and* — *Fennel*

Roasting carrots with a hint of sugar, vermouth and fennel seed brings out their natural sweet flavor. This dish is good warm or at room temperature.

8 SERVINGS   30% CALORIES FROM FAT   56 CALORIES PER SERVING

> 1 tablespoon olive oil
> 1¼ pounds small carrots (about 10), peeled
> 2 tablespoons sweet (red) vermouth or sherry, port or marsala
> 2 teaspoons sugar
> ½ teaspoon fennel seeds
> ¼ teaspoon salt
> ⅛ teaspoon freshly ground pepper

1. Preheat the oven to 400° F.

2. Line a small baking dish with foil, leaving plenty of overlap. Brush the olive oil onto the foil. Place the carrots in the center of the foil and sprinkle the vermouth, sugar, fennel, salt and pepper over the carrots.

3. Bring the edges of foil together and crimp to seal, adding an additional piece of foil, if necessary. Bake 15 to 20 minutes, or until the carrots are tender.

Green Beans Gourmandise with Tomato, Onion and Garlic

Flat pole beans, such as Italian green beans, have a robust flavor that works best for this dish, but any variety will do.

4 Servings   29% Calories from fat   104 Calories per serving

> *1 pound green beans*
> *1 tablespoon olive oil*
> *1 medium onion, cut into ½-inch dice*
> *2 garlic cloves, minced*
> *1 can (14 ounces) low-salt chopped tomatoes, drained*
> *⅛ teaspoon dried thyme leaves*
> *¼ teaspoon salt*
> *⅛ teaspoon freshly ground pepper*
> *1 tablespoon chopped parsley or basil*

1. In a large saucepan, cook the green beans in plenty of boiling water until they are still slightly crisp, 5 to 8 minutes. Drain in a colander and rinse under cold water. Drain well.

2. In a large nonstick skillet, heat the olive oil. Add the onion and garlic and cook over medium heat, stirring occasionally, until the onion is soft and lightly colored, 5 to 7 minutes.

3. Add the partially cooked green beans, the tomatoes, thyme, salt and pepper. Stir to mix with the onion and garlic. Cover and cook over medium-low heat 25 to 30 minutes, until the green beans are soft and the liquid is almost all evaporated.

4. Serve with the parsley sprinkled on top. Serve hot, at room temperature or chilled.

— *Braised Lettuce with Peas, Mint and Lemon* —

This unusual and highly refreshing vegetable combination goes particularly well with fish and chicken dishes. Leftovers can be pureed and turned into soup. Poached or roasted salmon with Hot Bacon and Calvados Dressing (page 71) is particularly delicious with this dish.

4 TO 6 SERVINGS   30% CALORIES FROM FAT   98 CALORIES PER SERVING

> *1 tablespoon olive oil*
> *2 large shallots, finely chopped*
> *1 medium head of Boston lettuce, quartered*
> *1 can (14½ ounces) reduced-sodium chicken broth*
> *Pinch of thyme*
> *½ teaspoon sugar*
> *1 bag (12 ounces) frozen peas, thawed*
> *Salt and freshly ground pepper*
> *1 tablespoon finely shredded mint leaves*
> *1 teaspoon grated lemon zest*

1. In a large nonstick skillet or flameproof casserole, heat the olive oil. Add the shallots and cook over medium heat until soft, 1 to 2 minutes. Add the lettuce, chicken broth, thyme and sugar. Simmer over medium heat 5 minutes, or until the lettuce is tender.

2. Add the peas and season with salt and pepper to taste. Cook 3 to 5 minutes longer, until the peas are heated through. Sprinkle the mint and lemon zest on top before serving.

Stuffed Baked Potatoes Cinderella

Potatoes Cinderella, or *Cendrillon*, got their name because they were origi-nally left in the ashes of the hearth to cook slowly before being stuffed. I frequently make a meal of one of these potatoes with a salad or a soup.

4 Servings   11% Calories from fat   172 Calories per serving

> *4 small baking potatoes (about 6 ounces each), scrubbed*
> *½ cup nonfat sour cream*
> *2 tablespoons grated Parmesan cheese*
> *2 tablespoons shredded Gruyère cheese*
> *2 tablespoons chopped chives*
> *½ teaspoon salt*
> *¼ teaspoon freshly ground pepper*

1. Preheat the oven to 400° F. Wrap each potato individually in aluminum foil and bake 45 to 60 minutes, or until the potatoes are cooked through and soft to the center.

2. In a small bowl, combine the sour cream, Parmesan cheese, Gruyère cheese, chives, salt and pepper.

3. When the potatoes are done and cool enough to handle, cut a wide lid out of each and set aside. Scoop out the potato, leaving a shell about ¼ inch thick.

4. Add the warm scooped-out potato to the sour cream mixture and mash and blend well. Stuff the mixture back into the potatoes and cover with the lids. (The recipe can be made to this point up to 12 hours ahead. Wrap and refrigerate.)

5. If made ahead, reheat the stuffed potatoes in a 375° F. oven 15 to 20 minutes, or longer if they have been refrigerated, until hot throughout. (They also reheat well in a microwave oven.)

Roasted Potato Slices with Garlic and Herbs

Though I like the texture of red potatoes here, any kind of thinly sliced unpeeled potato will work extremely well in this dish.

4 SERVINGS   26% CALORIES FROM FAT   125 CALORIES PER SERVING

1 pound small red potatoes, scrubbed and thinly sliced
1 tablespoon olive oil
1 teaspoon finely chopped garlic
¼ teaspoon dried thyme leaves
2 sprigs of fresh rosemary (optional; do not use dried rosemary for this dish)
¼ cup reduced-sodium chicken broth or water
½ teaspoon salt
¼ teaspoon freshly ground pepper

1. Preheat the oven to 400° F. In a medium bowl, combine the potatoes, olive oil, garlic, thyme, rosemary, chicken broth, salt and pepper. Toss to mix well.

2. Pour the contents of the bowl into a shallow baking dish or onto a baking sheet. Spread out the potato slices into a single layer. Cover the pan with foil and bake 45 minutes, or until the potatoes are tender.

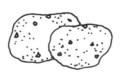

Potatoes Mashed with Spinach, Garlic and Cheese

This homey dish, called *truffade* in France, is from the Savoie in the mountainous eastern part of the country near Switzerland. I've lightened it up by removing the fat, while still preserving its comforting nature.

4 SERVINGS   24% CALORIES FROM FAT   178 CALORIES PER SERVING

1½ pounds baking potatoes (2 large), peeled and cut into 1-inch chunks
1 package (10 ounces) frozen chopped spinach
1 garlic clove, crushed through a press
½ cup shredded Gruyère or Swiss cheese (about 2 ounces)
Salt and freshly ground pepper

1. In a medium saucepan of boiling water, cook the potatoes until very tender, 10 to 12 minutes. Drain.

2. Meanwhile, cook the spinach according to the package directions until it is tender but still bright green. Drain and squeeze to remove as much liquid as possible.

3. In a medium bowl, mash the hot potatoes with a potato masher or fork; they should remain slightly lumpy. Mix in the spinach, garlic and cheese. Season with salt and pepper to taste. Serve or set aside at room temperature for up to 3 hours; reheat before serving.

Potato, Onion, and Tomato Gratin

This potato combination is a light and delicious side dish. I like to add a few ounces of crumbled goat cheese to the mixture, then enjoy the gratin with a salad as a meatless main course.

4 SERVINGS   36% CALORIES FROM FAT   172 CALORIES PER SERVING

> 1 tablespoon olive oil
> 1 pound medium red potatoes, peeled and thinly sliced
> 1 medium onion, thinly sliced
> 6 sprigs of fresh thyme or ¼ teaspoon dried thyme leaves
> ½ teaspoon salt
> ¼ teaspoon freshly ground pepper
> 1 can (14 ounces) low-salt chopped tomatoes, drained
> ½ cup dry white wine
> 2 ounces Gruyère cheese, shredded (about ½ cup)
> 1 tablespoon grated Parmesan cheese

1. Preheat the oven to 400° F. Brush an 8 × 11-inch baking dish or 10-inch gratin with the olive oil. Layer half of the potatoes in the dish. Scatter half the onion slices over the potatoes and season with the thyme, salt and pepper. Cover with half the tomatoes. Repeat these layers with the remaining potatoes, onion, thyme, salt, pepper and tomatoes.

2. Pour the wine into the dish and sprinkle the Gruyère and Parmesan cheese on top.

3. Bake 50 minutes, or until the potatoes are tender and all of the liquid is absorbed.

Potato Mousseline with Red and White Carrots

Parsnips, the "white carrots," add a splendid mellow flavor to this lightened version of mashed potatoes, while the carrots contribute an interesting crunchy texture. Serve with roast pork, beef or chicken.

4 to 6 Servings   5% Calories from fat   109 Calories per serving

2 large (1 pound) baking potatoes, peeled and cut into 1-inch chunks
2 medium (8 ounces) parsnips, peeled and cut into 1-inch pieces
1 can (14½ ounces) reduced-sodium chicken broth
½ cup nonfat milk
1 medium (4 ounces) finely grated peeled carrot
Salt and freshly ground pepper

1. In a medium saucepan, combine the potatoes, parsnips, chicken broth and enough water to cover the vegetables. Bring to a boil over high heat. Reduce the heat to medium and cook 15 to 20 minutes, or until the vegetables are tender.

2. Drain the potatoes and parsnips and empty them into a medium bowl. Add the milk and beat with an electric hand mixer until smooth. Stir in the carrot. Season with salt and pepper to taste and serve hot.

Baked Peppers Stuffed with Rice, Sausage and Tomatoes

4 SERVINGS   29% CALORIES FROM FAT   321 CALORIES PER SERVING

1 tablespoon olive oil
1 small onion, chopped
½ pound turkey or chicken sausages, removed from the casings and
*   crumbled*
1 teaspoon minced garlic
2 cups cooked rice
1 tablespoon chopped parsley
Pinch of thyme leaves
1 cup drained, canned low-salt chopped tomatoes, drained
4 large green bell peppers (about 6 ounces each)
1 can (14½ ounces) reduced-sodium chicken broth

1. Preheat the oven to 400° F. In a large nonstick skillet, heat the olive oil. Add the onion, sausage and garlic. Cook over medium heat, stirring occasionally, until the onion is tender, about 5 minutes.

2. Remove from the heat and add the cooked rice, parsley, thyme and tomatoes to the sausage mixture. Stir to blend well.

3. Cut the top off of each pepper and reserve. Leaving the peppers whole, cut out the seeds and trim out the white ribs from the insides. Divide the filling among the peppers and replace the tops of the peppers.

4. Place the peppers upright in a 9-inch square baking dish. Pour in the chicken broth and add enough water to reach halfway up the peppers. Cover the dish with foil and bake 1¼ hours, or until the peppers are just tender. Serve hot or cold.

Spinach with Lemon Confit and Olives

Spinach, lemon confit and olives is as light and tasty as it is attractive. Serve with fish and seafood as well as with poultry.

8 SERVINGS   30% CALORIES FROM FAT   110 CALORIES PER SERVING

1 tablespoon olive oil
2 pounds washed and trimmed fresh spinach leaves, ready to cook
½ recipe Lemon Confit (recipe follows)
12 Mediterranean-style or other oil-cured black olives, halved and pitted
Salt and freshly ground pepper

In a large nonstick skillet, heat the olive oil. Add the spinach gradually, cooking and stirring over high heat, until it wilts, 2 to 3 minutes. Mix in the lemon confit and olives. Season with salt and pepper to taste and serve.

Lemon Confit

Lemon confit is a delicious condiment, similar to a chutney or a relish, that can be served with seafood, fish, poultry, pork or lamb or with many vegetables and in salads.

16 SERVINGS   2% CALORIES FROM FAT   31 CALORIES PER SERVING

4 large lemons
½ cup sugar

1. Place the whole lemons in a medium nonreactive saucepan. Add enough water to cover. Bring to a boil and cook 15 minutes; drain.

2. In a small nonreactive saucepan, combine the sugar with 1 cup of water. Bring to a boil, stirring to dissolve the sugar. Reduce the heat and simmer 5 minutes.

3. Cut each lemon into 8 wedges and add to the sugar syrup. Simmer until the lemon skin is tender, about 15 minutes.

4. With a slotted spoon, remove the lemons to a wire rack and let cool. Cool the syrup in the pan. Place the lemon wedges in a covered container or jar and pour the cooled syrup over them. They will keep refrigerated about 2 weeks. Allow 2 wedges per serving.

— *Spinach with Parmesan Cheese and Pine Nuts* —

8 SERVINGS   45% CALORIES FROM FAT   52 CALORIES PER SERVING

1 tablespoon olive oil
2 pounds washed and trimmed fresh spinach leaves, ready to cook
2 tablespoons grated Parmesan cheese
¼ teaspoon salt
¼ teaspoon freshly ground pepper
1 tablespoon pine nuts (pignoli)

1. In a large nonstick skillet or flameproof casserole, heat the olive oil. Add the spinach gradually, turning and stirring until all of the leaves are just wilted, 2 to 3 minutes.

2. Remove from the heat and add the Parmesan cheese, salt, pepper and pine nuts. Toss and serve hot or at room temperature.

Ratatouille

Ratatouille is another multipurpose vegetable dish. Serve it cold with lemon slices and olives as an appetizer. Add chick peas and/or cooked white beans for a vegetarian entree, toss it with rice and bake it in a gratin, or enjoy a small bowl of it hot for a light lunch. Cooking all of the vegetables through "dry steaming" under foil brings out all of the flavors without adding any fat.

8 SERVINGS   6% CALORIES FROM FAT   54 CALORIES PER SERVING

1 large yellow bell pepper, thickly sliced
1 large green bell pepper, thickly sliced
2 medium onions, thickly sliced
2 medium zucchini, cut into 1-inch-thick slices
1 medium eggplant, cut into 1-inch dice
1 tablespoon finely chopped garlic
2 cans (14 ounces each) low-salt chopped tomatoes, drained
½ teaspoon dried thyme leaves
½ teaspoon salt
¼ teaspoon freshly ground pepper

1. Preheat the oven to 400° F. In a large bowl, combine all of the above ingredients. Stir until well mixed and empty into a large shallow baking dish or onto a large baking sheet.

2. Cover tightly with foil and bake 1½ hours in the oven, or until all of the vegetables are tender. Remove the foil and serve at once.

Julienne of Winter Root Vegetables

This colorful mixture of vegetables goes well with all meats, fish and sea-food. Leftovers make a welcome addition to a gratin or soup.

4 SERVINGS   30% CALORIES FROM FAT   104 CALORIES PER SERVING

2 medium carrots, peeled
2 medium turnips, peeled
1 medium parsnip, peeled
1 large leek (white part only)
1 tablespoon olive oil
1 teaspoon sugar
Pinch of grated nutmeg
1 tablespoon lemon juice
¼ teaspoon salt
⅛ teaspoon freshly ground pepper
1 tablespoon finely chopped parsley

1. Cut the carrots, turnips and parsnip into ¼-inch julienne strips on a mandoline or with the fine julienne blade of a food processor. Split the leek lengthwise in half and rinse well. Cut lengthwise again into ¼-inch-wide strips with a large sharp knife.

2. In a large nonstick skillet, heat the olive oil. Add the carrots, turnips, parsnip, leek, sugar, nutmeg, lemon juice, salt and pepper. Cover and cook over medium heat, stirring occasionally, about 5 minutes, until the vegetables are just tender. Serve hot, garnished with the parsley.

Vegetable Gratin with Tomatoes, Rice and Parmesan Cheese

Two cups of any cooked vegetable or vegetable mixture, such as ratatouille, eggplant, leeks, onion or squash, could be substituted for the zucchini-carrot mixture here. Serve as a side dish or as a light entree.

4 TO 6 SERVINGS   38% CALORIES FROM FAT   172 CALORIES PER SERVING

> *1 recipe Zucchini-Carrot Julienne with Garlic and Herbs (page 151)*
>   *or 2 cups of other cooked vegetable base*
> *1 cup cooked rice*
> *1 egg, beaten*
> *¼ teaspoon salt*
> *⅛ teaspoon freshly ground pepper*
> *1 tablespoon olive oil*
> *1 pound tomatoes (3 or 4 medium), thinly sliced*
> *2 tablespoons grated Parmesan cheese*

1. Preheat the oven to 400° F. In a medium mixing bowl, combine the zucchini-carrot mélange with the rice, egg, salt and pepper.

2. Brush the olive oil onto a 12-inch oval gratin or an 8 × 11-inch baking dish. Spread half of the vegetable-rice mixture into the dish. Layer half of the tomato slices on top. Repeat this one more time with the remaining ingredients.

3. Sprinkle the Parmesan cheese over the top and bake 45 minutes, or until golden and bubbly.

Tomatoes Provençal

Although vine-ripened summer tomatoes are best, excellent results can be had with fresh plum tomatoes, which are available most of the year. Tomatoes Provençal are delicious warm or cold. Leftover tomatoes are excellent chopped and spread on toasted bread.

8 SERVINGS   42% CALORIES FROM FAT   82 CALORIES PER SERVING

> *8 large plum tomatoes (about 2 pounds), halved lengthwise*
> *½ teaspoon salt*
> *¼ teaspoon freshly ground pepper*
> *2 tablespoons finely chopped garlic*
> *2 tablespoons finely chopped parsley*
> *½ cup unseasoned bread crumbs*
> *2 tablespoons olive oil*

1. Preheat the oven to 400° F. Place the tomatoes, cut side-up, in a shallow baking dish.

2. Sprinkle the salt, pepper, garlic, parsley and bread crumbs evenly over the tomatoes. Drizzle the olive oil over all.

3. Bake 10 to 15 minutes, or until the tomatoes are tender but not falling apart.

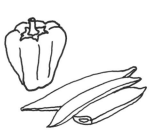

Roasted Onion Confit

Roasted onion confit is marvelous on its own as a vegetable with meats, fish and seafood. Serve it at room temperature with a few drops of sherry wine vinegar or as a condiment with sandwiches, salads, cold meats and fish.

4 TO 6 SERVINGS   26% CALORIES FROM FAT   100 CALORIES PER SERVING

4 large sweet yellow onions (about 2 pounds), thickly sliced
1 tablespoon finely chopped garlic
1 tablespoon olive oil
1 teaspoon sugar
½ teaspoon dried thyme leaves
1 bay leaf
½ teaspoon salt
¼ teaspoon freshly ground pepper

1. Preheat the oven to 400° F. Spread out the onion slices on a jelly roll pan. Add the garlic, olive oil, sugar, thyme, bay leaf, salt and pepper. Toss to mix well.

2. Cover the dish with foil and bake 50 to 60 minutes, or until the onions are very tender.

Roasted Zucchini Fans with Thyme

8 SERVINGS   62% CALORIES FROM FAT   24 CALORIES PER SERVING

4 medium zucchini (1 pound)
1 tablespoon olive oil
¼ cup reduced-sodium chicken broth or water
8 sprigs of fresh thyme or ½ teaspoon dried thyme leaves
¼ teaspoon salt
⅛ teaspoon freshly ground pepper

1. Preheat the oven to 400° F. Trim the zucchini and cut each in half lengthwise; then cut each crosswise in half. Make 4 equal lengthwise cuts down each piece to within ½ inch of one end (to hold the "fan" together).

2. Brush a large shallow baking dish with the olive oil and arrange the zucchini fans cut sides-down in a single layer. Pour the chicken broth over the zucchini and season with the thyme, salt and pepper.

3. Bake 8 to 12 minutes, or until the zucchini are tender.

Zucchini-Carrot Julienne with Garlic and Herbs

I learned to cook "shredded," or julienned, vegetables like this in Provence. At the time, the reason for cooking the vegetables quickly was to minimize heating up the kitchen on hot summer days. But now I find that this technique also allows vegetables to cook quickly with a minimum of fat, as it retains all of the flavor. Use a mandoline or the fine julienne blade or shredding blade of a food processor to complete the task.

4 SERVINGS   46% CALORIES FROM FAT   65 CALORIES PER SERVING

1 tablespoon olive oil
4 small carrots (½ pound), shredded or cut into fine julienne strips
2 medium zucchini, shredded or cut into fine julienne strips
1 teaspoon finely chopped garlic
½ teaspoon salt
¼ teaspoon freshly ground pepper
1 tablespoon chopped parsley
1 tablespoon finely shredded fresh basil leaves

1. In a large nonstick skillet, heat the olive oil. Add the carrots, zucchini and garlic, cover and cook over medium heat, stirring occasionally, 5 minutes, or until just tender.

2. Season with the salt and pepper. Stir in the parsley and basil and serve.

Zucchini Barquettes Filled with Olives, Onion and Tomato

Zucchini barquettes belong to a family of Provençal dishes known as *petits farcis* ("little stuffed things"). Vegetables such as zucchini, onion, tomatoes, peppers and small eggplant can be treated in a similar fashion. A selection of *petits farcis* are often served as an hors d'oeuvre or as a vegetable side dish with roasted or grilled chicken and meat.

8 SERVINGS   41% CALORIES FROM FAT   71 CALORIES PER SERVING

> 4 small zucchini (about 6 inches long) or 2 large, halved crosswise
> 1 tablespoon olive oil
> 1 medium onion, chopped
> 1 garlic clove, minced
> 1 cup canned low-salt chopped tomatoes, drained
> ½ cup plain bread crumbs
> 12 oil-cured Mediterranean black olives, pitted and chopped
> 1 tablespoon chopped parsley
> ¼ teaspoon dried thyme leaves
> ⅛ teaspoon salt
> ⅛ teaspoon freshly ground pepper
> ¼ cup reduced-sodium chicken broth

1. Preheat the oven to 400° F. Halve each zucchini lengthwise and hollow out a cavity in each piece, leaving a ⅜-inch shell. Coarsely chop the scooped-out zucchini and set aside.

2. In a large nonstick skillet, heat the olive oil. Add the chopped zucchini, onion and garlic. Cover and cook over medium heat, stirring occasionally, 10 minutes, or until tender. Add the tomatoes and cook, covered, 5 minutes longer.

3. Uncover and stir in the bread crumbs, olives, parsley, thyme, salt and pepper. Remove from the heat and let cool.

4. Stuff the zucchini halves with the filling and place in a shallow baking dish. Pour the chicken broth into the baking dish. Bake 30 minutes, or until the zucchini halves are tender.

Chapter Seven

PASTA,
RICE
AND
BEANS

Some of the most comforting of all French dishes are those based on pasta, rice and beans. Pasta is not generally eaten as a separate course in France as it is in Italy; it is usually served as a main course by itself or as a side dish. Plain noodles often accompany stews. Some of the best-known pasta dishes from the South of France are actually Italian influenced, but they have a unique French twist. For instance, Thin Noodles with Pistou and Roasted Tomato are based on the Italian pesto sauce, but the roasted thyme-scented tomatoes is a Provençal touch. Because I have lightened the pistou to include only a minimum of olive oil and grated cheese, the dish is very light and low in fat.

I have included two rice dishes that are particularly delicious, practical and lean. Provençal Lemon Herb Rice can be enjoyed warm or cold. It is lovely stuffed into vegetables, tossed with some cold seafood as a light salad or mixed into a gratin or a soup. Red Rice with Tomatoes, Onion and Cheese is a wonderful side dish that can easily be converted into a light, one-dish meal by mixing in some leftover pieces of chicken or fish and some cooked vegetables.

Another dish the French and Italians share a fondness for are gnocchi. Classic French gnocchi are made from a *panade,* or paste, of flour, water and butter and are usually served with tomato sauce. Provençal gnocchi are more imaginative and light. Made with a minimum of flour and no butter at all, they are almost entirely derived from potatoes, zucchini or pumpkin. Because the gnocchi rely on the natural binding of potato or squash, they incorporate very little flour.

Couscous is a Moroccan specialty that has been wholeheartedly adopted by the French. The two variations included in this book are based on vegetables and some fish and seafood poached in broth. If butter is omitted in preparing the actual couscous grain (which is semolina, just like pasta), the dish is actually very calorie affordable.

Red Beans, Chicken and Pumpkin Piperade is an inspired, nutritious and utterly delicious light entree. Enjoy it with or without chicken. It is also excellent served chilled as a side dish.

Finally, I have developed a version of White Beans Cassoulet Style in which the fat has been kept down to a minimum: A tiny bit of bacon, which gives it that wonderful smoky taste, is blanched to remove excess fat and salt. And the carrots, onions and celery base are gently "foil sautéed" (see page 17) until the vegetables are tender and caramelized. These beans are so robust it's hard to believe that this is a lightened version. Cassoulet-style beans are used on page 123 to create a main-course cassoulet; they are superb as a side vegetable, chilled as an appetizer, as a soup base, and tempting just on their own, baked with some bread crumbs, as a light entree with a simple green salad.

Gratin of Macaroni, Tomatoes and Chèvre

Rice, orzo or couscous are interchangeable in this recipe. Serve with roast lamb, pork or beef, or as a light meatless meal with a salad.

4 TO 6 SERVINGS   30% CALORIES FROM FAT   326 CALORIES PER SERVING

> *2 cups elbow macaroni or other small tubular pasta*
> *1 pound tomatoes, preferably plum, cut into ½-inch dice*
> *¼ teaspoon dried thyme leaves*
> *4 ounces goat cheese, crumbled*
> *3 garlic cloves, finely chopped*
> *1 tablespoon finely shredded basil (optional)*
> *1 tablespoon chopped parsley*
> *½ teaspoon salt*
> *¼ teaspoon freshly ground pepper*
> *1 tablespoon olive oil*
> *1 cup reduced-sodium chicken broth*
> *½ cup plain bread crumbs*

1. Preheat the oven to 400° F. In a large saucepan of boiling salted water, cook the macaroni until tender but still firm, 6 to 8 minutes. Drain into a colander.

2. In a medium bowl, combine the cooked macaroni with the tomatoes, thyme, goat cheese, garlic, basil, parsley, salt and pepper. Toss to mix well.

3. Coat a 12-inch gratin or 8 × 11-inch baking dish with the olive oil and empty the macaroni mixture into the dish. Pour in the chicken broth and sprinkle the bread crumbs evenly over the top.

4. Bake the gratin 25 to 30 minutes, or until the top is golden brown and crusty.

Thin Noodles with Pistou and Roasted Tomatoes

4 TO 6 SERVINGS   19% CALORIES FROM FAT   364 CALORIES PER SERVING

2 pounds plum tomatoes, halved lengthwise
3 garlic cloves, minced
½ teaspoon salt
¼ teaspoon freshly ground pepper
1 tablespoon chopped parsley
1 tablespoon fresh thyme leaves or ½ teaspoon dried
1 tablespoon olive oil
12 ounces capellini or spaghettini
Pistou (page 53)
2 tablespoons grated Parmesan cheese

1. Preheat the oven to 400° F. Place the tomatoes, cut side-up, in a shallow baking dish large enough to hold them in a single layer. Sprinkle the garlic over the tomatoes and season with the salt, pepper, parsley and thyme. Drizzle the olive oil over the tomatoes.

2. Cover the pan with aluminum foil and bake about 15 minutes, or until the tomatoes are tender. Remove the foil and let stand until the tomatoes cool off enough to handle.

3. Pour any pan juices from the tomatoes into a bowl. Peel the tomatoes and coarsely chop them. Add the tomatoes, along with any juice they give off, to the bowl. (The roasted tomato sauce can be made ahead. Set aside at room temperature for up to 3 hours.)

4. In a large pot of boiling salted water, cook the pasta until tender but still firm, 6 to 8 minutes.

5. Meanwhile, in a nonreactive medium saucepan, combine the roasted tomato sauce with the Pistou and the Parmesan cheese. Bring to a simmer over medium heat, stirring occasionally. Drain the pasta and transfer to a large bowl. Pour the sauce over the pasta, toss and serve.

Thin Noodles with Fondue de Tomates

This is a recipe made for soft, ripe summer tomatoes. They literally melt in the pan for a few minutes and are ready to serve. *Fondue de tomates* is another sauce that shouldn't just be reserved for pasta dishes; spoon it over fish and vegetables.

4 Servings   13% Calories from fat   397 Calories per serving

> 1 tablespoon extra virgin olive oil
> 2 garlic cloves, thinly sliced
> 2 pounds ripe tomatoes, coarsely chopped
> 1 tablespoon chopped parsley
> 1 tablespoon finely shredded basil
> 1 tablespoon chopped chives
> ½ teaspoon salt
> ¼ teaspoon freshly ground pepper
> 12 ounces capellini or spaghettini

1. In a large nonstick skillet, heat the olive oil over medium heat. Add the garlic and cook until it begins to take on a light golden color, 1 to 2 minutes. Add the chopped tomatoes, raise the heat to high and bring to a boil.

2. Remove the pan from the heat, stir well and let the tomatoes "melt" in the hot oil. Set aside until the tomatoes are just warm to the touch. Mix in the parsley, basil, chives, salt and pepper.

3. Bring a large pot of salted water to a boil. Add the capellini and cook until tender but still firm, 6 to 8 minutes. Drain and transfer to a large bowl. Pour the tomato sauce over the pasta, toss and serve.

Vermicelli Nests with Clams, Spinach, Tomato and Fresh Thyme

Long before I ever sampled the Italian *spaghetti con vongole,* I was smitten by the French *palourdes en nids* ("clams in their nests"). Try to use the smallest, sweetest clams for this dish.

6 SERVINGS   12% CALORIES FROM FAT   371 CALORIES PER SERVING

1 tablespoon extra virgin olive oil
1 tablespoon finely chopped garlic
4 dozen clams (littlenecks, cherrystones or manilla), scrubbed
1 cup dry white wine
2 teaspoons fresh thyme leaves or ½ teaspoon dried
½ pound spinach, washed, trimmed and cut into thin strips
1 pound plum tomatoes, seeded and chopped
Freshly ground pepper
12 ounces vermicelli or capellini

1. In a large flameproof casserole, heat the olive oil. Add the garlic and cook over medium-low heat until the garlic begins to soften, 2 to 3 minutes.

2. Add the clams and toss with the garlic. Pour in the wine and add the thyme. Raise the heat to high and bring to a boil. Cover the pan and cook over medium-high heat until all the clams open, 5 to 7 minutes. (Discard any that do not open.) Add the spinach and tomatoes, toss and remove from the heat. Season with pepper to taste.

3. Meanwhile, in a large pot of boiling salted water, cook the pasta until just tender but still firm, 5 to 7 minutes. Drain and immediately arrange the pasta in small piles, or "nests," in the bottom of 4 individual soup or pasta bowls.

4. Divide the clams among the bowls. Pour the remaining broth and vegetables over all and serve at once.

Couscous with Vegetables and Harissa

Couscous of any kind was always a special treat in my family. There was so much ritual and lore attached to its production that for a long time I thought I'd never be able to duplicate it over here. As it turns out, couscous is exceedingly easy to prepare and can be low in calories, too. This vegetable couscous is excellent on its own or as a base for chicken. Leftovers can be used as a vegetable side dish or a soup.

6 SERVINGS   6% CALORIES FROM FAT   376 CALORIES PER SERVING

> *1 medium red onion, cut into ½-inch dice*
> *2 medium carrots, peeled and thinly sliced*
> *2 small turnips, peeled and cut into ½-inch dice*
> *1 can (14½ ounces) reduced-sodium chicken broth*
> *1 cup diced (½-inch) peeled and seeded pumpkin or hubbard or*
> *   butternut squash*
> *1 medium zucchini, thinly sliced*
> *¼ pound green beans, cut into 1-inch lengths*
> *1 medium leek (white and tender green), well rinsed and thinly sliced*
> *1 can (14 ounces) low-salt chopped tomatoes*
> *1 cup canned chick peas, preferably low-salt, drained*
> *2 tablespoons raisins or currants*
> *2 cups instant couscous*
> *1 tablespoon chopped cilantro*
> *Harissa Sauce (page 108)*

1. In a large stew pot, bring the red onion, carrots, turnips, chicken broth and 4 cups of water to a boil. Reduce the heat and simmer 15 minutes. Add the squash, zucchini, green beans, leek, tomatoes, chick peas and raisins and continue cooking until the vegetables are tender, 15 to 20 minutes longer.

2. Meanwhile, cook the couscous according to the directions on the package.

3. Mound the couscous in the center of a large serving bowl. Ladle the vegetables and some of the broth over all. Garnish with the chopped cilantro and pass the Harissa Sauce on the side.

Couscous Marinière

Seafood couscous is a dish of North African origin that is appreciated by Sicilians as well as the French. It makes a festive, spectacular-looking party dish—one that can be enjoyed without guilt.

6 SERVINGS   14% CALORIES FROM FAT   379 CALORIES PER SERVING

1 medium onion, cut into ½-inch dice
2 medium carrots, peeled and cut into ½-inch dice
6 garlic cloves, chopped
1 cup diced (½-inch) peeled and seeded pumpkin or hubbard or
    butternut squash
2 cans (14½ ounces each) reduced-sodium chicken broth or vegetable
    broth
1 medium zucchini, thinly sliced
1 can (14 ounces) low-salt chopped tomatoes, drained
1 can (14 ounces) low-salt chick peas, drained
½ teaspoon saffron threads, dissolved in ¼ cup hot water
¼ teaspoon salt
¼ teaspoon freshly ground pepper
1 pound thick, skinned and boned chunks of assorted fish: monkfish,
    swordfish, sea bass and/or cod
12 mussels, scrubbed and debearded
6 sea scallops
6 large shrimp, shelled and deveined
3 cups hot cooked couscous
1 tablespoon chopped cilantro
Harissa Sauce (page 108)

1. In a large stew pot, bring the onion, carrots, garlic, pumpkin and chicken broth to a boil. Reduce the heat and simmer 15 minutes.

2. Add the zucchini, tomatoes, chick peas, saffron, salt and pepper and continue cooking until all the vegetables are just barely tender, about 5 minutes.

3. Add the assorted fish to the simmering base and cook 5 minutes. Add the mussels, cover and cook until they just begin to open, 2 to 3 minutes. Add the scallops and shrimp and continue cooking until the shrimp are pink and loosely curled and the mussels are open, 2 to 3 minutes. (Discard any mussels that do not open.)

4. Mound the couscous on a large, deep serving platter and ladle the vegetables, fish and seafood with some of the broth over it. Sprinkle the cilantro on top and pass the Harissa Sauce on the side.

Provençal Lemon Herb Rice

This is one of the most practical and delicious of rice dishes. It can be served warm or at room temperature and it can be added to soups or mixed in with salads or stuffed into vegetables. Leftovers also serve as a base for Provençal gratins known as *tians*.

4 SERVINGS   22% CALORIES FROM FAT   159 CALORIES PER SERVING

> *¾ cup long-grain white rice*
> *1 tablespoon extra virgin olive oil*
> *1 tablespoon reduced-sodium chicken broth*
> *2 tablespoons finely chopped herbs, such as parsley, basil and/or mint*
> *1 tablespoon lemon juice*
> *½ teaspoon grated lemon zest*
> *Salt and freshly ground pepper*

1. In a small saucepan, bring 1½ cups water to a boil over high heat. Add the rice, cover and reduce the heat to low. Simmer 20 minutes, or until the rice is tender and all the water is absorbed.

2. In a medium bowl, whisk together the olive oil, chicken broth, chopped herbs, lemon juice and lemon zest. Add the hot rice to the bowl and mix well. Season with salt and pepper to taste.

— *Red Rice with Tomatoes, Onion and Cheese* —

6 SERVINGS   19% CALORIES FROM FAT   167 CALORIES PER SERVING

1 tablespoon extra virgin olive oil
1 medium onion, chopped
1 large garlic clove, minced
1 cup long-grain white rice
1 can (14 ounces) low-salt chopped tomatoes
1 can (14½ ounces) reduced-sodium chicken broth
Salt and freshly ground pepper
2 tablespoons grated Parmesan cheese
1 tablespoon finely shredded basil

1. In a medium saucepan, heat the olive oil. Add the onion and garlic, cover and cook over medium heat 2 minutes. Uncover and cook, stirring often, until soft but not brown, about 3 minutes longer.

2. Add the rice and toss to coat it evenly. Cook, stirring, 1 to 2 minutes. Pour in the tomatoes and chicken broth. Bring to a boil, cover and reduce the heat to low. Cook, stirring occasionally, 20 to 25 minutes, until all of the liquid has been absorbed and the rice is tender.

3. Season with salt and pepper to taste. Turn into a serving bowl and sprinkle the Parmesan cheese and basil on top.

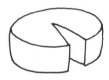

— *Pumpkin Gnocchi Gratin with Tomato Sauce* — *and Two Cheeses*

Gnocchi are also a French favorite. Made from raw pumpkin, these gnocchi are exceptionally light and have a pleasant crisp texture.

4 SERVINGS   7% CALORIES FROM FAT   185 CALORIES PER SERVING

> *1 pound pumpkin or hubbard or butternut squash, peeled, seeded and*
> *   cut into 1-inch pieces*
> *1 cup flour*
> *½ teaspoon grated nutmeg*
> *½ teaspoon salt*
> *¼ teaspoon freshly ground pepper*
> *2 egg whites*
> *1½ cups tomato sauce*
> *1 tablespoon grated Parmesan cheese*
> *1 tablespoon shredded Gruyère cheese*

1. Using the shredding blade on a food processor, grate the pumpkin. Empty the contents into a bowl and replace the shredding blade with the steel blade in the processor. Return the shredded pumpkin to the machine and puree, pulsing on and off, until smooth. Add the flour, nutmeg, salt, pepper and egg whites and mix well.

2. Divide the dough into 12 balls 2 inches in diameter; an ice cream scoop dipped in warm water works well. (The dough should be slightly tacky, but if it is too sticky to handle easily, dust it with a small amount of flour.)

3. In a flameproof casserole, bring 3 inches of slightly salted water to a boil. Drop the gnocchi into the water, reduce the heat to medium-low and simmer until they float to the top, 15 to 18 minutes. Remove with a slotted spoon and drain on a clean kitchen towel. (The recipe can be made ahead to this point. Let the gnocchi cool, then transfer them to a plate, cover and refrigerate for up to 2 days until ready to use.)

4. Preheat the oven to 400° F. Place the gnocchi in a medium gratin dish. Pour the tomato sauce over the gnocchi and sprinkle the Parmesan and Gruyère cheese over the top.

5. Bake 20 to 30 minutes, or until golden and bubbly.

— *Red Beans, Chicken and Pumpkin Piperade* —

Piperade is a Basque spicy tomato, pepper and onion mélange. In this version, other typical Basque staples such as pumpkin and red beans are added to make a dish that is reminiscent of chili. While it contains very little meat—only one-half pound of chicken for four people, there is additional protein in the beans, and the piperade is substantial enough to be served as a main course.

4 SERVINGS   9% CALORIES FROM FAT   193 CALORIES PER SERVING

1 can (14 ounces) low-salt chopped tomatoes, with their juice
1 medium onion, thinly sliced
1 medium green bell pepper, thinly sliced
1 cup diced (½-inch) peeled and seeded pumpkin or hubbard or
    butternut squash
2 garlic cloves, minced
¼ teaspoon salt
⅛ teaspoon freshly ground pepper
½ teaspoon cayenne pepper
1 teaspoon sugar
1 tablespoon red wine vinegar
1 can (14 ounces) low-salt red beans, rinsed and drained
½ pound skinless, boneless chicken breast, cut into thin strips
1 ounce prosciutto, trimmed of all fat and cut into thin strips
1 tablespoon chopped parsley

1. In a medium stew pot, combine the tomatoes, onion, bell pepper, squash and garlic. Bring to a boil. Lower the heat to medium-low and simmer until the vegetables are just tender, about 20 minutes.

2. Season the stew with the salt, pepper, cayenne, sugar and vinegar. Add the beans and chicken and simmer 10 to 15 minutes longer.

3. Turn into a serving dish and sprinkle the prosciutto and parsley over the top.

White Beans Cassoulet Style

Cassoulet beans have many uses as a vegetable or as a soup base or stew. For a completely vegetarian approach, omit the bacon and use canned vegetable broth instead of the chicken broth.

10 Servings   16% Calories from fat   172 Calories per serving

> *2 cups Great Northern white beans, rinsed and picked over*
> *1 strip of lean bacon, chopped*
> *1 tablespoon olive oil*
> *1 medium onion, cut into ½-inch dice*
> *2 medium carrots, peeled and cut into ½-inch dice*
> *1 large celery rib, cut into ½-inch dice*
> *½ cup dry white wine*
> *1 can (14½ ounces) reduced-sodium chicken broth*
> *8 garlic cloves, chopped*
> *1 bay leaf*
> *4 sprigs of parsley*
> *4 sprigs of fresh thyme or ¼ teaspoon dried thyme leaves*
> *6 whole black peppercorns*
> *1 can (14 ounces) low-salt chopped tomatoes, with their juice*

1. Put the beans in a large saucepan and add enough cold water to cover by at least 1 inch. Bring to a boil, reduce the heat and simmer 10 minutes. Remove from the heat and let stand 45 minutes; drain.

2. Meanwhile, bring a small saucepan of water to a boil. Add the bacon and cook 30 seconds. Drain and rinse briefly under running water. Pat dry.

3. Preheat the oven to 375° F. In a large, heavy stew pot (with an oven-proof cover), heat the olive oil. Add the bacon, onion, carrots and celery. Press a sheet of aluminum foil right down on the vegetables and cook over medium-low heat, stirring occasionally, until the vegetables are tender and the onion is golden, 7 to 10 minutes.

4. Add the beans, wine, chicken broth, 2 cups of water, the garlic, bay leaf, parsley, thyme, peppercorns and tomatoes. Make sure there's enough liquid to cover the ingredients by 1 inch; if not, add some more broth or water.

5. Bring to a boil on top of the stove. Cover and place in the oven. Bake 1½ hours, or until the beans are tender. Check the pot from time to time during cooking to make sure there's enough liquid left. Add additional broth or water if necessary.

Chapter Eight

DESSERTS

Contrary to what you might think, the art of French *pâtisserie,* or pastry making, in all of its spun-sugar glory, is really only reserved for special occasions. In France, dessert is typically a piece of cheese or fruit, finished off with a glass of wine. Most French country desserts are based on fruits: fruit salads, marinated fruits, baked fruits, fruit tarts, fruit mousses, fruit soufflés and frozen fruit sorbets.

In this chapter, I have divided the recipes into four main categories: Cold fruit desserts, warm baked fruit desserts, frozen desserts and the classics revisited. The fruit desserts consist of classic combinations, such as Macedoine of Fruit, Peach Parfait with Blueberries, White Wine and Crème de Cassis and Grapefruit, Melon and Mint Coupe with Sauternes.

Warm baked Fruit Gratin with Sugar Nut Crust, Roasted Fig Confit with Thyme and Honey and Clafoutis with Red Fruits are quintessential homey French desserts—comforting and surprisingly easy on the waistline. Naturally low in calories, light fresh sorbets are a popular dessert option. I've developed a Frozen Strawberry Cream that uses no cream, but nonfat vanilla yogurt instead, and a wicked chocolate velvet sorbet that derives its silkiness from Dutch cocoa and its lightness from nonfat milk. The Lemon Sorbet with Cassis is tart and refreshing, the Plum Sorbet à l'Orange, with its lovely purple color, is intensely flavored. Both are exceptionally low-calorie, no-fat treats.

Adapting classic desserts to the lightened format was indeed challenging. The trick was to maintain their traditional flavor, texture and look while knocking out the calories and cholesterol. This can be especially difficult in pastry making, since results are based on strict proportions and crucial chemical reactions. The results of these desserts, I hope you'll agree, was well worth the effort.

Apple Galette with Honey, Lemon and Thyme is a paper thin, country-style tart, whose intense apple flavor on a crisp, buttery crust is a sheer delight. Here the crust is made with a small amount of butter, and the apples are sweetened with just a hint of honey. Pear Soufflé with Raspberry Coulis is a real showstopper. The soufflé relies on the natural thickening properties and flavor of the pears and doesn't contain any flour, egg yolks or cream. Lastly—and most decadently—I offer you a culinary contradiction of terms: a light Chocolate Mousse. This rich-tasting mousse is made without a drop of cream, butter or egg yolks, yet it is so creamy, you'll swear it isn't so.

Apple Galette with Honey, Lemon and Thyme

Apple galette was the first thing I ever learned to cook at the age of four. This is the easiest and homiest of all French apple tarts. A thin layer of apple provides intense fruit flavor, and a thin, thin crust beneath provides just the right amount of buttery crust. The thyme is an authentic touch, but you can omit it if you prefer.

8 SERVINGS   38% CALORIES FROM FAT   150 CALORIES PER SERVING

> *1 teaspoon light olive oil*
> *4 tablespoons chilled butter, cut into small pieces*
> *1 cup all-purpose flour*
> *Pinch of salt*
> *¼ cup plus 1 tablespoon ice water*
> *2 large baking apples, such as Golden Delicious, peeled, cored and*
> *   sliced paper thin*
> *2 tablespoons honey*
> *1 tablespoon lemon juice*
> *3 sprigs of fresh thyme or ¼ teaspoon dried thyme leaves*

1. Preheat the oven to 400° F. Brush the olive oil into a thin film on a cookie sheet that has no sides.

2. In a food processor, pulse the butter, flour and salt together until a coarse meal forms. Add the water and process only until the dough begins to form a ball. Flatten the dough ball into a thick even disk. Cover with plastic wrap and refrigerate at least 30 minutes.

3. Roll out the dough directly on the oiled cookie sheet into a 13-inch circle. In a medium bowl, toss the apples, honey and lemon juice. Arrange the apples slices in a single layer in slightly overlapping concentric circles, leaving a 1-inch border all around. Fold the dough border over the apples to form a rustic edge on the tart. Pour any remaining lemon-honey juice from the bowl over the apples and sprinkle the thyme on top.

4. Bake 1 hour, or until the crust is golden and the apples are tender. Serve warm.

Chilled Apple Mousse with Warm Caramelized Apples and Nuts

The combinations of hot and cold and soft and crunchy and sweet and tart in this dessert are beguiling. Soft, cold apple mousse contrasts with the hot apple slices and nuts. Notice I use two types of apples here for a more complex flavor.

8 SERVINGS   9% CALORIES FROM FAT   147 CALORIES PER SERVING

> 2 tablespoons slivered almonds
> 2½ pounds sweet baking apples (such as Golden Delicious), peeled, cored and chopped
> 2 tablespoons apricot preserves
> 3 tablespoons Calvados or rum
> 4 egg whites
> Pinch of salt
> 2 tablespoons plus 1 teaspoon sugar
> 2 medium (½ pound total) tart cooking apples (such as Granny Smith), peeled, cored and thinly sliced

1. Preheat the oven to 325° F. Spread out the almonds in a small baking dish and toast in the oven about 5 minutes, until fragrant and very lightly browned. Immediately transfer to a small dish and set aside.

2. In a large nonstick skillet, cook the chopped apples and apricot preserves over medium heat, covered, 15 minutes, or until the apples are soft. Stir every few minutes to prevent scorching.

3. Remove from the heat and mash the apples with a fork until they are coarsely pureed. Let cool to room temperature. Then stir in the Calvados.

4. In a clean, dry medium bowl, beat the egg whites with the salt until foamy. Add 1 teaspoon sugar and continue beating until stiff, glossy peaks form. Fold the egg whites into the cooled apple base and pour into a glass serving bowl. Cover and refrigerate at least 2 hours, or until well chilled.

5. Shortly before serving, heat the remaining 2 tablespoons sugar in a large nonstick skillet. Add the apple slices and toasted almonds and cook, stirring, until the apples begin to brown.

6. Pour the hot apple slices over the chilled mousse and serve immediately.

Chocolate Mousse

Deadly, habit-forming and decadent are all terms that might describe this chocolate mousse. Yet it contains no butter, no cream and no egg yolks! But you would never know it. Who could imagine that a dessert this light could be so intense? Because the chocolate flavor is so important to this dish, I recommend using only the best semisweet or bittersweet Belgian, French or Swiss chocolate. You will taste the difference.

6 TO 8 SERVINGS   34% CALORIES FROM FAT   136 CALORIES PER SERVING

> *4½ ounces semisweet or bittersweet chocolate*
> *1 tablespoon unsweetened cocoa powder, preferably Dutch*
> *3 tablespoons hot espresso or strongly brewed coffee*
> *8 egg whites*
> *Pinch of salt*
> *¼ cup sugar*

1. In a double boiler over simmering water, combine the chocolate, cocoa powder and hot coffee. Cook, stirring, until the chocolate is melted and the mixture is smooth, 7 to 10 minutes. Remove the chocolate base from the heat.

2. In a large, clean and dry bowl, beat the egg whites with the salt until foamy. Add the sugar and continue beating until they are stiff and glossy.

3. Mix ¼ of the egg whites thoroughly into the chocolate base to lighten it. Add the lightened chocolate back into the remaining egg whites and fold just until no trace of white remains. Pour the mousse into a large soufflé dish or 6 to 8 smaller individual ones.

4. Refrigerate at least 1 hour but no more than 6 hours before serving. (After 8 hours the egg whites will begin to break down and cause the mousse to "weep" some liquid in the bottom of the dish.)

Clafoutis with Red Fruits

Clafoutis is a country fruit dessert that lies somewhere between a custard and a cake. I've lightened the original recipe by cutting down on egg yolks, sugar, butter and flour. Applesauce thickens and moisturizes without contributing a lot of calories, while the egg whites add lightness. Clafoutis can be made with many different varieties of fruits, such as strawberries, raspberries, blueberries, grapes, plums or cherries. It is best enjoyed warm.

6 TO 8 SERVINGS   13% CALORIES FROM FAT   104 CALORIES PER SERVING

> 1 teaspoon butter
> 1 egg yolk
> ½ cup sweetened applesauce
> ¼ cup sugar
> ¼ cup all-purpose flour
> ¼ cup nonfat milk
> ½ teaspoon almond extract
> 4 egg whites
> Pinch of salt
> 2 cups mixed strawberries, raspberries and pitted cherries (any one or
>   in combination)

1. Preheat the oven to 350° F. Use the butter to grease a 9-inch round pie pan.

2. In a medium bowl, beat the egg yolk. Mix in the applesauce, sugar, flour, milk and almond extract.

3. In another bowl, beat the egg whites until frothy. Add the salt and beat until stiff but not dry. Fold the egg whites into the applesauce mixture and pour into the prepared pie pan. Drop the fruit into the batter; do not press it down.

4. Bake 20 minutes, or until the clafoutis is golden and puffy and a toothpick inserted into the center comes out clean.

— *Roasted Fig Confit with Thyme and Honey* —

Figs are one of the most sensuous and delicious of all fruits. In this dish they are simply roasted with thyme, a fragrant herb, honey and a touch of wine until they are almost soft enough to spread. Roasted figs can be enjoyed warm or cold. They are excellent as a topping for ice milk or—one of my favorites—spread on toast for breakfast.

4 Servings   25% Calories from fat   131 Calories per serving

1 tablespoon extra virgin olive oil
6 large fresh figs (about ¾ pound), halved
2 tablespoons fragrant honey, such as wildflower
2 tablespoons dry red wine
4 sprigs of fresh thyme or ¼ teaspoon dried thyme leaves

1. Preheat the oven to 375° F. Brush an 8- or 9-inch baking dish with the olive oil and arrange the figs in the dish, cut side-down, in a single layer.

2. Pour the honey and wine over the figs and top with the thyme. Cover with a sheet of aluminum foil.

3. Bake 10 to 15 minutes, or until the figs are soft and tender.

Fruit Gratin with Sugar Nut Crust

Croquant, the French word for this topping, means "crunchy." Indeed, the dish is very much like our own fruit crisps. Try it with other fruits, such as apples, mixed berries, nectarines or cherries; they are especially good in combinations. If you really want to splurge, try this dessert with a small (2-ounce) scoop of vanilla ice milk, at an added 46 calories.

6 SERVINGS   30% CALORIES FROM FAT   180 CALORIES PER SERVING

1 teaspoon butter, softened
3 large peaches, thinly sliced
5 large red plums, thinly sliced
¼ cup sugar
2 tablespoons butter, cut into small bits
¼ cup all-purpose flour
2 tablespoons chopped almonds

1. Preheat the oven to 375° F. Grease a 9-inch square baking dish or pie plate with the butter.

2. In a small bowl, toss together the peaches and plums and empty them into the prepared baking dish.

3. In the same small bowl, combine the sugar, butter, flour and nuts together. Toss and pinch with your fingers until the mixture resembles coarse meal. Sprinkle the topping evenly over the top of the fruit and press down gently.

4. Bake 45 minutes, or until the fruit is tender and the topping is golden and bubbling. Serve hot or at room temperature.

Macedoine of Fruit

Refreshing, simple and very light, this marinated mixed fruit salad is one of the most common of all French home-style desserts. In the summer, this salad can be enjoyed over and over again, taking on slightly different flavors each time, depending on what fruits happen to be on hand. In addition to those listed in the recipe, melons, strawberries, raspberries, blueberries, grapefruit and plums all work well. Flavor the salad with any kind of liqueur, brandy, *eau de vie* or white wine. For a real treat, try combining leftover fruit salad with plain nonfat yogurt in a blender for a cooling liquid lunch on a hot summer day.

6 Servings   3% Calories from fat   143 Calories per serving

> 2 medium apples, peeled, cored and thinly sliced
> 2 large bananas, thinly sliced
> 1 tablespoon lemon juice
> 1 can (8 ounces) unsweetened pineapple chunks, with their juice
> 1 large peach or nectarine, thinly sliced
> 1 cup seedless red grapes
> 2 large oranges, peeled and sectioned
> ¼ cup orange juice, preferably fresh
> 1 tablespoon Grand Marnier, Triple Sec or other orange liqueur

1. In a medium bowl, toss the apples and bananas with the lemon juice. Add the pineapple, pineapple juice, peach, grapes, orange sections, orange juice and orange liqueur. Toss to mix well.

2. Cover with plastic wrap and refrigerate, tossing occasionally, at least 1 hour, or until well chilled.

Apple Soufflé Cake

This "cake" always receives raves. It has an unusual moist texture and is actually a fallen soufflé, just like many of the popular chocolate mousse cakes we all enjoy. I developed this dessert by lightening up an old French recipe for *pâté de pommes*, which is a more cakelike dessert. Serve with Raspberry Coulis (page 179) for extra-special occasions.

8 SERVINGS   8% CALORIES FROM FAT   145 CALORIES PER SERVING

1 teaspoon butter, softened
¼ cup plus 2 tablespoons sugar
1 cup sweetened applesauce
2 to 3 medium-size tart-sweet cooking apples (such as Granny Smith), peeled, cored and shredded to yield 1 cup
1 egg yolk
¼ teaspoon almond extract
½ cup all-purpose flour
6 egg whites
Pinch of salt
2 tablespoons apricot preserves
2 tablespoons Calvados, applejack or rum

1. Preheat the oven to 325° F. Use the butter to grease a 9-inch springform pan. Dust the bottom and sides of the pan with 2 tablespoons of the sugar.

2. In a medium bowl, combine the applesauce, shredded apples, egg yolk and almond extract. Mix well. Sprinkle the flour on top and fold in.

3. In a clean, dry bowl, whip the egg whites with the salt until foamy. Add the remaining ¼ cup sugar and beat until stiff, glossy peaks are formed.

4. Mix ¼ of the beaten egg whites into the apple base to lighten the mixture. Then fold in the rest of the egg whites. Pour the batter into the prepared springform pan.

5. Bake 45 minutes to 1 hour, or until golden and puffed and a toothpick inserted in the center comes out clean. Remove the pan to a wire rack and let cool about 10 minutes, until the cake pulls away from the sides of the pan. (The cake will fall as it cools.)

6. Meanwhile, in a small saucepan, combine the apricot preserves with the Calvados. Cook over medium heat, stirring, until hot and melted, about 2 minutes.

7. Invert the cake to unmold it onto a serving plate. Brush the apricot glaze over the warm cake. Let cool completely, then refrigerate until chilled before serving.

— *Peach Parfait with Blueberries, White Wine* — *and Crème de Cassis*

More often than not, meals in France end with a piece of fruit and a glass of wine. Peaches, blueberries, wine and crème de cassis, layered in a tall glass dish, raise this homey combination to a dessert elegant enough for a dinner party.

4 SERVINGS   3% CALORIES FROM FAT   225 CALORIES PER SERVING

> *4 small peaches, thinly sliced*
> *2 cups blueberries or blackberries*
> *2 cups dry white wine*
> *¼ cup crème de cassis*

Alternate layers of peaches and blueberries in 4 glass parfait dishes, champagne flutes or wine goblets. Pour some wine into each and top with cassis.

Pear Soufflé with Raspberry Coulis

This pear soufflé with raspberry *coulis,* or puree, is a spectacular dessert you'll want to serve to company. I sometimes call this dish "pear air," which describes just how light and smooth it is. This soufflé can be assembled through step 6 up to 2 hours ahead of time; cover and refrigerate until ready to bake. Do not let the soufflé sit any longer, or it will collapse during baking.

8 to 10 Servings   4% Calories from fat   223 Calories per serving

> 2 teaspoons butter, softened
> 1/3 cup plus 3 tablespoons sugar
> 2 cans (29 ounces each) pear halves in heavy syrup, drained
> Minced zest and 1 tablespoon juice from 1 orange
> 2 teaspoons cornstarch
> 1/4 cup Poire William or other pear eau de vie or kirsch or brandy
> 8 large egg whites
> Pinch of salt
> Raspberry Coulis (recipe follows)

1. Preheat the oven to 425° F. Use the butter to grease the bottom and sides of a 2-quart soufflé dish. Sprinkle 2 tablespoons of the sugar inside the dish and rotate until it lightly coats the sides and bottom. Pour out any excess.

2. Cut 2 pear halves into 1/4-inch dice and set aside. In a food processor, blend together 1/3 cup of the sugar and the orange zest. Add the remaining pears and puree until smooth.

3. Pour the pear puree into a medium saucepan and cook over medium heat, stirring often, 20 to 30 minutes, or until the base is thickened and reduced to about 1½ cups.

4. In a small bowl, dissolve the cornstarch in the 1 tablespoon orange juice and add to the cooked pears. Cook over medium heat until the mixture boils and thickens, about 5 minutes longer. Pour into a bowl and let cool to room temperature. Then stir in the pear brandy.

5. In a large, clean bowl, beat the egg whites with the salt until foamy. Add the remaining 1 tablespoon sugar and continue beating until stiff, glossy peaks form. Mix ¼ of the egg whites thoroughly into the cooked pear base to lighten the mixture. Then fold in the remaining whites just until blended; do not overmix.

6. Spoon half of the soufflé mixture into the prepared dish. Sprinkle half of the diced pears evenly over the soufflé base. Add the remaining soufflé mixture and top with the remaining diced pears.

7. Bake 15 minutes, or until well puffed and golden. Serve immediately, spooning 2 tablespoons of raspberry coulis over each portion.

Raspberry Coulis

Raspberry *coulis* is an intensely flavored, all-purpose dessert sauce. Try it anywhere you might use the custard-based *crème anglaise* or whipped cream. Raspberry coulis also makes a very fine topping for ice milk.

MAKES ABOUT 1 CUP   1% CALORIES FROM FAT   18 CALORIES PER TABLESPOON

> *1 package (10 ounces) frozen raspberries packed in heavy syrup, thawed, juices reserved*
> *1 tablespoon lemon juice*

1. In a food processor, puree the raspberries with their syrup and the lemon juice until smooth.

2. For a finer texture, if you like, press the coulis through a fine strainer to remove the seeds.

Grapefruit, Melon and Mint Coupe with Sauternes

One of the most perfect light desserts one can ingest is a chilled glass of Château d'Yquem Sauternes. If you ever have the opportunity—and the pocketbook—do try this unique taste sensation. There are, however, many lesser-known, inexpensive and delicious Sauternes or other dessert wines that will work in this recipe. Sauternes is traditionally poured into a chilled melon half for dessert. I have also found that grapefruit is another fruit that complements this wine. Enjoy this variation on a classic wine-tasting theme.

4 SERVINGS   2% CALORIES FROM FAT   187 CALORIES PER SERVING

> 4 medium grapefruits, peeled and sectioned
> 2 cups diced (1-inch) melon, such as honeydew or cantaloupe
> 2 cups Sauternes or other dessert wine
> 1 tablespoon finely shredded fresh mint leaves

1. In a medium glass bowl, combine the grapefruit sections, melon, Sauternes and mint leaves. Toss to mix.

2. Cover with plastic wrap and refrigerate at least 1 to 2 hours, until chilled, before serving.

Sorbet au Chocolat Velours

In keeping with its name, the texture of this intense chocolate sherbet is smooth as velvet. Cocoa powder has all of the great flavor of solid chocolate, but without the fat. I suggest using only the best, pure Dutch process unsweetened cocoa for the best results. For a real treat, serve with a tablespoon or two of raspberry coulis on top.

4 TO 6 SERVINGS   16% CALORIES FROM FAT   158 CALORIES PER SERVING

1 cup unsweetened cocoa powder, preferably Dutch
¹/₂ cup sugar
Pinch of salt
2 cups nonfat milk
¹/₂ teaspoon vanilla extract

1. In a medium saucepan, combine the cocoa, sugar and salt. Slowly whisk in the milk.

2. Bring to a boil, stirring constantly, over medium heat. Reduce the heat to low and continue cooking and stirring 5 minutes longer.

3. Remove from the heat and let cool for 10 to 15 minutes. Then stir in the vanilla. Pour into a bowl, cover with plastic wrap and refrigerate until the mixture is thoroughly cold.

4. Freeze in an ice cream maker according to the manufacturer's directions or follow the directions on page 184 for Food Processor Frozen Desserts.

Lemon Sorbet with Cassis

Lemon sorbet, softened in flavor with a bit of orange, is a light, clean, refreshing way to end a meal. This recipe works with any citrus fruit. Try it with lime or pink grapefruit as well.

4 SERVINGS   1% CALORIES FROM FAT   101 CALORIES PER SERVING

¼ cup lemon juice
½ cup orange juice
¼ cup sugar
1 teaspoon minced lemon zest
¼ cup water
1 egg white
2 tablespoons crème de cassis

1. In a medium mixing bowl, combine the lemon juice, orange juice, sugar, lemon zest and water. Stir to dissolve the sugar. Cover and refrigerate, stirring from time to time, 2 to 3 hours, until well chilled.

2. In a clean, dry bowl, beat the egg white until stiff. Fold the beaten egg white into the chilled citrus mixture. Turn into an ice cream maker and freeze according to the manufacturer's directions, or follow the directions on page 184 for Food Processor Frozen Desserts. After completing step 3, add the beaten egg white and process until smooth.

3. Scoop the sorbet into 4 dessert dishes. Pour ½ tablespoon of the crème de cassis over each and serve at once.

Plum Sorbet à l'Orange

The lovely deep purple color of this sorbet is just beautiful. You may want to serve 1 scoop of this sorbet with 1 scoop of the Lemon Sorbet with Cassis (page 182), or the Sorbet au Chocolate Velours (page 181).

4 SERVINGS   2% CALORIES FROM FAT   177 CALORIES PER SERVING

½ pound purple or red plums, halved, pitted and cut into ½-inch dice
½ cup water
½ cup orange juice
½ cup sugar
2 tablespoons kirsch or brandy
1 tablespoon lemon juice
1 tablespoon crème de cassis
½ teaspoon minced lemon zest
Pinch of cinnamon

1. In a medium nonreactive saucepan, bring the plums, water, orange juice and sugar to a boil over medium heat, stirring to dissolve the sugar. Cook until the plums are tender, about 10 minutes. Remove from the heat and let cool to room temperature.

2. In a food processor or blender, puree the plum mixture. Add the kirsch, lemon juice, cassis, lemon zest and cinnamon and mix until blended.

3. Transfer to a covered container and refrigerate the mixture 2 to 3 hours, or until totally cold.

4. Freeze in an ice cream maker according to the manufacturer's directions or follow the directions on page 184 for Food Processor Frozen Desserts.

Frozen Strawberry Cream

Yogurt replaces heavy cream in this frozen desert, but it doesn't lessen the delicious creaminess and intense strawberry flavor of the dish.

4 TO 6 SERVINGS   2% CALORIES FROM FAT   208 CALORIES PER SERVING

2 pints ripe strawberries, stemmed and sliced (2 cups)
2 pints nonfat vanilla yogurt
1 tablespoon sugar

1. Puree 1 cup of the strawberries in a blender or food processor. Blend in the yogurt.

2. In a medium bowl, toss the remaining strawberries with the sugar. Add the strawberry yogurt and stir gently to mix.

3. Cover and refrigerate 2 hours, until chilled. Then freeze in an ice cream maker according to the manufacturer's directions or follow the directions on page 184 for Food Processor Frozen Desserts.

Food Processor Frozen Desserts

1. Pour the finished base into a small rectangular metal baking pan or into 2 metal ice cube trays.

2. Freeze the base until solid.

3. Just before serving, cut the base into 1-inch cubes. Place the cubes in a food processor and process until smooth. Serve immediately.

Index

Almond(s)
  chilled apple mousse with warm
    caramelized apples and, 170
  sugar crust, fruit gratin with, 174
Anchovy(-ies)
  roasted red peppers marinated with
    capers, olives and, 34
  sauce, grilled tuna with, 89
Apple
  desserts
    galette with honey, lemon and thyme,
      169
    mousse, chilled, with warm
      caramelized apples and nuts, 170
    soufflé cake, 176
  watercress and endive salad, with
    Roquefort cheese and roasted walnut
    dressing, 62
Artichokes
  à la barigoule with tomatoes and thyme,
    131
  stuffed Niçoise style, 21
Arugula, endive and beets with roasted
  walnut dressing, 62
Asparagus
  and endive and orange salad with
    raspberry vinaigrette, 61
  with sherry Dijon dressing, 22
  Maltaise, 22

Bacon
  about, 16
  and Calvados dressing, hot, potato and
    frisée salad with, 71
  warm roasted salmon salad with
    mesclun, potato, onion and, 74
Basil, fresh, shrimp and scallop brochettes
  with, 91
Bean(s)

red, chicken and pumpkin piperade, 164
white
  cassoulet of lamb, pork, sausage and,
    123
  cassoulet style, 165
Beef
  steak au poivre, 122
  poached, vegetables and broth
    (pot-au-feu), 120
Beets
  and arugula and endive with roasted
    walnut dressing, 62
  and endive, watercress and onion salad
    with lemon-garlic dressing, 64
  with raspberry vinegar, 23
Belgian endive. See Endive
Blueberries, peach parfait with white wine,
  crème de cassis and, 177
Bouillabaisse, 104
  of clams, spinach, potato and saffron
    broth, 106
Bread, toasted garlic, 51
Bread crumbs, about, 15
Broths, about, 16

Cabbage
  red, chiffonade of, 24
  savoy, chiffonade of, 134
Capers
  roasted red peppers marinated with
    olives, anchovies and, 34
  smoked fish salad with pickled red
    onions, spinach and, 73
Carrot(s)
  Provençal with sweet vermouth and
    fennel, 135
  red and white, potato mousseline with,
    142
  salad, shredded sweet and sour, 24
  soup, creamy, 46

-zucchini julienne with garlic and herbs, 151

Cassoulet
style white beans, 165
of white beans, lamb, pork and sausage, 123

Champagne vinaigrette
cucumbers with mint and, 27
cumin, 77

Cheese(s). *See also* Chèvre; Feta cheese;
Gruyère cheese; Parmesan
cheese about, 15
potatoes mashed with spinach, garlic and, 140
pumpkin gnocchi gratin with tomato sauce and two, 163
Roquefort, apple watercress and endive salad with roasted walnut dressing and, 62

Chèvre (goat cheese)
gratin of macaroni, tomatoes and, 155
roasted, mesclun salad with, 70
spread, herbed, 26
with cucumbers and lemon honey dressing, 26

Chicken
breasts
"diable," grilled, 113
Niçoise, 114
Provençal, 111
salad with sherry shallot dressing, warm, 68
sauté au vinaigre, 116
sauté chasseur, 115
with tarragon, mushrooms and wine, foil-steamed, 119
coq au vin, 112
in a pot grandmere, 117
and red beans and pumpkin piperade, 164

Chiffonade
of red cabbage, 24
savoy cabbage, 134

Chocolate
mousse, 171
sorbet au, velours, 181

Choucroute garnie marinière, 96

Citrus "cooked" salmon on a bed of fresh herbs, 40

Clafoutis with red fruits, 172

Clams
bouillabaisse of spinach, potato, saffron broth and, 106

vermicelli nests with spinach, tomato, fresh thyme and, 158

Confit
fig, 173
garlic, 132
lemon, 144
spinach with olives and, 144
roasted onion, 150
shallot, pan-roasted duck breasts à l'orange with, 118

Coq au vin, 112

Corsican tomato, cucumber, mint and feta salad, 67

Coulis
raspberry, 179
pear soufflé with, 178
red pepper, 96
baked sole roulades with zucchini and, 95

Couscous
marinière, 160
with vegetables and harissa, 159

Crème de cassis
lemon sorbet with, 182
peach parfait with blueberries, white wine and, 177

Croutons, herbed, 48
chilled tomato soup with mint, feta cheese and, 48

Cucumber(s)
barquettes filled with tapenade, 28
herbed chèvre spread with lemon honey dressing and, 26
with mint and champagne vinaigrette, 27
soup, chilled, 47
tomato, mint and feta salad, Corsican, 67

Cumin champagne vinaigrette, 77

Dijon vinaigrette, 36
poached leeks with plum tomatoes and, 29

Dip, eggplant caviar, 30

Dressing. *See also* Vinaigrette
hot bacon and Calvados, potato and frisée salad with, 71
lemon Dijon yogurt, green bean and hazelnut salad with, 66
lemon-garlic, beet, endive, watercress and onion salad with, 64
lemon honey, herbed chèvre spread with cucumbers and, 26

lemon honey-date, hearts of romaine with, 72
sherry Dijon, asparagus with, 22
  Maltaise, 22
sherry shallot, 69
roasted walnut, 63
  apple, watercress and endive salad with Roquefort cheese and, 62
  arugula, endive and beets with, 62
Duck breasts à l'orange with shallot confit, pan-roasted, 118

Eggplant caviar, 30
Endive salad
  apple, watercress and, with Roquefort cheese and roasted walnut dressing, 62
  arugula, beets and, with roasted walnut dressing, 62
  asparagus, orange and, with raspberry vinaigrette, 61
  beet, watercress, onion and, with lemon-garlic dressing, 64

Fennel
  orange and olive salad with Gruyère cheese and, fresh, 65
  roasted pork loin with garlic, tomato and, 125
Fennel seeds, carrots Provençal with sweet vermouth and, 135
Feta cheese
  chilled tomato soup with mint, herbed croutons and, 48
  tomato, cucumber and mint salad, Corsican, 67
Fig confit with thyme and honey, roasted, 173
Fish. See also Halibut; Red snapper; Salmon; Shellfish; Sole; Tuna
  bouillabaisse, 104
  choucroute garnie marinière, 96
  couscous, 160
  monkfish "gigot" with thyme, roasted, 101
  salmon trout, poached, with aromatic vegetables, 100
  smoked, salad with capers, pickled red onions and spinach, 73
  swordfish with harissa sauce, grilled paillard of, 107

Foil "roasting," about, 17
Foil "sauté," about, 17
Food processor frozen desserts, 184
Frisée and potato salad with hot bacon and Calvados dressing, 71
Frozen strawberry cream, 184
Fruit(s). See also specific fruits
  clafoutis with red, 172
  gratin, with sugar nut crust, 174
  macedoine of, 175

Garlic
  bread
    chapons, 30
    toasted, 51
  confit, 132
  green beans gourmandise with tomato, onion and, 136
  -lemon dressing, beet, endive, watercress and onion salad with, 64
  -lemon vinaigrette, 64
  potatoes mashed with spinach, cheese and, 140
  puree, sweet, 133
  roasted pork loin with fennel, tomato and, 125
  roasted potato slices with herbs and, 139
  roasted whole, with fresh thyme, 25
  zucchini-carrot julienne with herbs and, 151
Gnocchi, pumpkin, gratin with tomato sauce and two cheeses, 163
Goat cheese. See Chèvre
Grapefruit, melon and mint coupe with Sauternes, 180
Gratin
  of macaroni, tomatoes and chèvre, 155
  potato, onion and tomato, 141
  pumpkin gnocchi, with tomato sauce and two cheeses, 163
  vegetable, tomatoes, rice and Parmesan cheese, 148
Green bean(s)
  gourmandise with tomato, onion and garlic, 136
  and hazelnut salad with lemon Dijon yogurt dressing, 66
Green peas. See Pea(s)
Gruyère cheese, fresh fennel, orange and olive salad with, 65

Halibut
    en papillote with lemon, 83
    steaks with herbed citrus vinaigrette,
        roasted, 84
Harissa sauce, 108
    couscous with vegetables and, 159
    grilled paillard of swordfish with, 107
Hazelnut and green bean salad with
    lemon Dijon yogurt dressing, 66
Herb(s,-ed)
    about, 14
    chèvre spread, 26
        with cucumbers and lemon honey
            dressing, 26
    chilled tomato soup with mint, feta
        cheese and, 48
    citrus vinaigrette, 85
    croutons, 48
    fresh, citrus "cooked" salmon on a bed
        of, 40
    rice, Provençal lemon, 161
        roasted potato slices with garlic
            and, 139
        zucchini-carrot julienne with garlic
            and, 151
Honey
    apple galette with lemon, thyme
        and, 169
    lemon dressing, herbed chèvre spread
        with cucumbers and, 26
    roasted fig confit with thyme and, 173
Horseradish sauce, 121

Lamb
    cassoulet of white beans, pork, sausage
        and, 123
    roasted leg of, with olives, 124
Leek(s)
    poached, with plum tomatoes and Dijon
        vinaigrette, 29
    and potato soup, 49
Lemon
    apple galette with honey, thyme and,
        169
    confit, 144
        spinach with olives and, 144
    Dijon yogurt dressing, 66
        green bean and hazelnut salad
            with, 66
    -garlic dressing with beet, endive,
        watercress and onion salad, 64
    -garlic vinaigrette, 64

herb rice, Provençal, 161
honey dressing, herbed chèvre spread
    with cucumbers and, 26
sorbet with cassis, 182
Lentils, marinated, 32
    roasted salmon with sherry wine vinegar
        and, 87
Lettuce. *See also* Mesclun
    Boston, with peas, mint and lemon,
        braised, 137
    hearts of romaine with lemon honey-
        date dressing, 72
    sweet pea and mint soup, 54

Macaroni, gratin of tomatoes, chèvre
    and, 155
Macedoine of fruit, 175
Meaux mustard sauce, broiled salmon
    paillard with, 88
Melon, grapefruit and mint coupe with
    Sauternes, 180
Mesclun
    grilled shrimp with roasted orange
        thyme vinaigrette and, 78
    salad with roasted chèvre, 70
    warm roasted salmon salad with potato,
        onion, bacon and, 74
Mint
    braised lettuce with peas, lemon
        and, 137
    chilled tomato soup with herbed
        croutons, feta cheese and, 48
    cucumbers with champagne vinaigrette
        and, 27
    and grapefruit and melon coupe with
        Sauternes, 180
    salad of tomato, cucumber and feta,
        Corsican, 67
    and sweet pea and lettuce soup, 54
Monkfish "gigot" with thyme, roasted,
    101
Mousse
    apple, chilled, with warm caramelized
        apples and nuts, 170
    chocolate, 171
    shrimp and scallop, with watercress
        cream, 92
Mushroom(s)
    foil-steamed chicken breasts with
        tarragon, wine and, 119
    wild
        and field mushroom salad, mixed, 33

ragout tartines, 38
Mussels marinière steamed with wine and aromatic vegetables, 86
Mustard
sauce, Meaux, broiled salmon paillard with, 88
tarragon sauce, roasted rabbit with, 128

Noodles
thin
with fondue de tomates, 157
with pistou and roasted tomatoes, 156
zucchini, 103
Nut(s). *See* Almond(s); Walnut dressing, roasted
hazelnut and green bean salad with lemon Dijon yogurt dressing, 66
pine, spinach with Parmesan cheese and, 145

Oils, about, 15
Olive(s)
fresh fennel and orange salad with Gruyère cheese, 65
roasted leg of lamb with, 124
roasted red peppers marinated with capers, anchovies and, 34
spinach with lemon confit and, 144
zucchini barquettes filled with onion, tomato and, 152
Onion(s)
confit, roasted, 150
gratin of potato, tomato and, 141
green beans gourmandise with tomato, garlic and, 136
red, pickled, 31
smoked fish salad with capers, spinach and, 73
red rice with tomatoes, cheese and, 162
salad
beet, endive watercress, and, with lemon-garlic dressing, 64
potato and, marinated, 36
soup, gratinéed, 50
warm roasted salmon salad with mesclun, potato, bacon and, 74
watercress and potato soup: soupe à la cressionière, 57
zucchini barquettes filled with olives, tomato and, 152

Orange
asparagus and endive salad with raspberry vinaigrette, 61
broiled sole à l', 102
and fresh fennel and olive salad with Gruyère cheese, 65
pan-roasted duck breasts à l', with shallot confit, 118
Oysters with 3 mignonette sauces, 41

Parfait with blueberries, white wine and crème de cassis, peach, 177
Parmesan cheese
red rice with tomatoes, onion and, 162
spinach with pine nuts and, 145
vegetable gratin with tomatoes, rice and, 148
Parsnips, in potato mousseline with red and white carrots, 142
Pea(s)
braised lettuce with mint, lemon and, 137
lettuce and mint soup, 54
Peach parfait with blueberries, white wine and crème de cassis, 177
Pear soufflé with raspberry coulis, 178
Pepper, black, about, 14
Pepper(s), sweet green
stuffed with rice, sausage and tomatoes, baked, 143
Pepper(s), sweet red, roasted, 34
coulis, 96
baked sole roulades with zucchini and, 95
marinated with capers, olives and anchovies, 34
poached scallop salad with champagne cumin vinaigrette and, 76
Pine nuts, spinach with Parmesan cheese and, 145
Piperade, red beans, chicken and pumpkin, 164
Pistou, 53
soupe au, 52
thin noodles with roasted tomatoes and, 156
Plum sorbet à l'orange, 183
Pork
cassoulet of white beans, lamb, sausage and, 123
loin, roasted, with fennel, garlic and tomato, 125

Potato(es)
Cinderella, stuffed baked, 138
and frisée salad with hot bacon and
Calvados dressing, 71
and leek soup, 49
mashed with spinach, garlic and
cheese, 140
mousseline with red and white
carrots, 142
and onion and tomato gratin, 141
and onion salad, marinated, 36
slices with garlic and herbs, roasted, 139
warm roasted salmon salad with
mesclun, onion, bacon and, 74
and watercress and onion soup: soupe à
la cressionière, 57
Pot-au-feu (poached beef, vegetables and
broth), 120
Poulet. *See also* Chicken
Provençal, 111
sauté au vinaigre, 116
sauté chasseur, 115
Provençal marinated vegetable sandwich,
37
Pumpkin
gnocchi gratin with tomato sauce and
two cheeses, 163
and red beans and chicken piperade,
164

Rabbit with tarragon mustard sauce,
roasted, 128
Raifort, sauce au, 121
Raspberry
coulis, 179
pear soufflé with, 178
vinaigrette, asparagus, endive and
orange salad with, 61
vinegar, beets with, 23
Ratatouille, 146
Red snapper
Catalane, baked, 98
goujonettes à la barigoule, 99
Rice
baked peppers stuffed with sausage,
tomatoes and, 143
Provençal lemon herb, 161
red, with tomatoes, onion and
cheese, 162
vegetable gratin with tomatoes,
Parmesan cheese and, 148
and zucchini soup, 58

Roquefort cheese, apple, watercress and
endive salad with roasted walnut
dressing and, 62
Rouille, 105

Saffron, bouillabaisse of clams, spinach,
potato, and, 106
Salad dressing. *See* Dressing; Vinaigrette
Salade Niçoise, 75
Salmon
on a bed of fresh herbs, citrus
"cooked," 40
paillard with Meaux mustard sauce,
broiled, 88
rillettes, 39
salad with mesclun, potato, onion and
bacon, warm roasted, 74
with sherry wine vinegar and marinated
lentils, roasted, 87
Salmon trout, poached, with aromatic
vegetables, 100
Salt, about, 15
Sandwich, Provençal marinated vegetable,
37
Sauerkraut, in choucroute garnie
marinière, 96
Sausage
baked peppers stuffed with rice,
tomatoes and, 143
cassoulet of white beans, lamb, pork
and, 123
Sauternes, grapefruit, melon and mint
coupe with, 180
Scallop(s)
baked with garlic, tomatoes, wine and
bread crumbs, 94
salad with champagne cumin vinaigrette
and roasted red peppers, poached, 76
and shrimp brochettes with fresh
basil, 91
and shrimp mousse with watercress
cream, 92
Shellfish. *See also* Clams; Scallop(s);
Shrimp
bouillabaisse, 104
choucroute garnie marinière, 96
couscous, 160
mussels marinière steamed with wine
and aromatic vegetables, 86
Sherry
Dijon dressing, asparagus with, 22
shallot dressing, 69

warm chicken breast salad with, 68

Shrimp
"à la nage" with spinach and vegetable julienne, 90
with roasted orange thyme vinaigrette and mesclun, grilled, 78
and scallop brochettes with fresh basil, 91
and scallop mousse with watercress cream, 92

Sole
à l'orange, broiled, 102
roulades with zucchini and red pepper coulis, baked, 95

Sorbet
au chocolat velours, 181
lemon, with cassis, 182
plum, à l'orange, 183

Soufflé(s)
cake, apple, 176
pear, with raspberry coulis, 178

Spices, about, 14

Spinach
bouillabaisse of clams, potato, saffron broth and, 106
with lemon confit and olives, 144
with Parmesan cheese and pine nuts, 145
potatoes mashed with garlic, cheese and, 140
smoked fish salad with capers, pickled red onions and, 73
and vegetable julienne, shrimp "à la nage" with, 90
vermicelli nests with clams, tomato, fresh thyme and, 158

Spread, herbed chèvre, 26
with cucumbers and lemon honey dressing, 26

Steak au poivre, 122

Stew
bouillabaisse, 104
of clams, spinach, potato and saffron broth, 106
pot-au-feu (poached beef, vegetables and broth), 120
veal, merengo, 126

Sweet peas. See Pea(s)

Swordfish with harissa sauce, grilled paillard of, 107

Tapenade, cucumber barquettes filled with, 28

Tarragon
foil-steamed chicken breasts with mushrooms, wine and, 119
mustard sauce, roasted rabbit with, 128

Technique, about, 17

Thickening, about, 17

Thyme
apple galette with honey, lemon and, 169
artichokes à la barigoule with tomatoes and, 131
fresh, roasted whole garlic with, 25
grilled veal paillard with, 127
with monkfish "gigot," roasted, 101
roasted fig confit with honey and, 173
roasted zucchini fans with, 150
vermicelli nests with clams, spinach, tomato and fresh, 158

Tomato(es)
artichokes à la barigoule with thyme and, 131
baked peppers stuffed with rice, sausage and, 143
cucumber, mint and feta salad, Corsican, 67
gratin of macaroni, chèvre and, 155
gratin of potato, onion and, 141
green beans gourmandise with onion, garlic and, 136
persillade, 35
plum, poached leeks with Dijon vinaigrette and, 29
Provençal, 149
red rice with onion, cheese and, 162
roasted, thin noodles with pistou and, 156
roasted pork loin with fennel, garlic and, 125
sauce
fondue de tomates, thin noodles with, 157
pumpkin gnocchi gratin with two cheeses and, 163
scallops baked with garlic, wine, bread crumbs and, 94
soup with mint, herbed croutons and feta cheese, chilled, 48
vegetable gratin with rice, Parmesan cheese and, 148

vermicelli nests with clams, spinach, fresh thyme and, 158

zucchini barquettes filled with olives, onion and, 152

Tuna
  with anchovy sauce, grilled, 89
  cucumber barquettes filled with tapenade, 28
  salade Niçoise, 75

Veal
  paillard with thyme, grilled, 127
  stew merango, 126
Vegetable(s). *See also specific vegetables*
  aromatic
    mussels marinière steamed with wine and, 86
    poached salmon trout with, 100
  beef and broth, poached (pot-au-feu), 120
  couscous with harissa and, 159
  gratin with tomatoes, rice and Parmesan cheese, 148
  ratatouille, 146
  sandwich, Provençal marinated, 37
  soup
    au pistou, 52
    potage santé, chunky, 56
    puree of garden, 55
    white winter root, 45
  and spinach julienne, shrimp "à la nage" with, 90
  winter root, julienne of, 147
Vermicelli nests with clams, spinach, tomato and fresh thyme, 158
Vermouth, sweet, carrots Provençal with fennel and, 135
Vinaigrette
  champagne, cucumbers with mint and, 27
  champagne cumin, 77
    poached scallop salad with roasted red peppers and, 76
  Dijon, 36
    poached leeks with plum tomatoes and, 29
  herbed citrus, 85
    roasted halibut steaks with, 84
  lemon-garlic, 64
  raspberry, asparagus endive and orange salad with, 61

roasted orange thyme, 79
  grilled shrimp with mesclun and, 78
Vinegar
  about, 15
  raspberry, beets with, 23

Walnut dressing, roasted, 63
  apple, watercress and endive salad with Roquefort cheese and, 62
  arugula, endive and beets with, 62
Watercress
  cream, 93
    shrimp and scallop mousse with, 92
  and potato and onion soup: soupe à la cressionière, 57
  salad
    apple, endive and, with Roquefort cheese and roasted walnut dressing, 62
    beet, endive, onion, and, with lemon-garlic dressing, 64
Wine, white
  foil-steamed chicken breasts with tarragon, mushrooms and, 119
  mussels marinière steamed with aromatic vegetables and, 86
  peach parfait with blueberries, crème de cassis and, 177
  Sauternes, grapefruit, melon and mint coupe with, 180
  scallops baked with garlic, tomatoes, bread crumbs and, 94
Wines and spirits, about, 16

Zucchini
  baked sole roulades with red pepper coulis and, 95
  barquettes filled with olives, onion and tomato, 152
  -carrot julienne with garlic and herbs, 151
  fans with thyme, roasted, 150
  noodles, 103
  and rice soup, 58